BOOK FIVE

Navigating Achievement for Struggling Students with the Common Core State Standards

BOOK FIVE

Navigating Achievement for Struggling Students with the Common Core State Standards

Tom Hierck | Brian McNulty | Linda A. Gregg

Chris Weber | Lillian A. Hawkins | Polly Patrick

Deborah M. Telfer | Mary F. Piper | Angela Peery

LEAD+
LEARN
PRESS

ENGLEWOOD, COLORADO

The Leadership and Learning Center
317 Inverness Way South, Suite 150
Englewood, Colorado 80112
Phone 1.866.399.6019 | Fax 303.504.9417
www.leadandlearn.com

Published by Lead + Learn Press, a division of Houghton Mifflin Harcourt.

Library of Congress Cataloging-in-Publication Data
Hierck, Tom, 1960-
    Navigating achievement for struggling students with the common core state standards / Tom Hierck, Brian McNulty, Linda A. Gregg, Chris Weber, Lillian A. Hawkins, Polly Patrick, Deborah M. Telfer, Mary F. Piper, Angela Peery.
        pages cm. — (Getting ready for the common core handbook series ; book five)
    Includes bibliographical references and index.
    ISBN 978-1-935588-44-3 (alk. paper)
    1. Education—Standards—United States. 2. Children with disabilities—Education—United States. 3. Learning disabled children—Education—United States. 4. Response to intervention (Learning disabled children) 5. Academic achievement—United States. 6. Learning strategies—United States. I. Title.
    LB3060.83.H54 2014
    371.90973—dc23
                                                                                2014000372

ISBN 978-1-935588-44-3

Printed in the United States of America

01 02 03 04 05 06   19 18 17 16 15 14

4500477391   A B C D E F G

Contents

List of Exhibits

About the Authors

Thomas Hierck is a Professional Development Associate with The Leadership and Learning Center. He has been an educator since 1983 in a career that has spanned all grade levels and many roles in public education. His experiences as a teacher, administrator, district leader, department of education project leader, and executive director have provided a unique context for his education philosophy.

Tom's most recent publication (with coauthors Charlie Coleman and Chris Weber), *Pyramid of Behavior Interventions: Seven Keys to a Positive Learning Environment*, examines the inextricable link between behavior and academics as educators work to unlock the potential that resides in all students. He has also contributed chapters to the Tom Guskey–edited *Teacher as Assessment Leader* and *Principal as Assessment Leader* and published two books that celebrate the role of the teacher, *What Do You Make?* and *I Am the Future*.

Tom's dynamic presentations explore the importance of positive learning environments and the role of assessment to improve student learning. His belief that "every student is a success story waiting to be told" has led him to work with teachers and administrators to create positive school cultures and build effective relationships that facilitate learning for all students. His work for The Center echoes these beliefs.

Tom and his wife, Ingrid, are the proud parents of three grown children and grandparents of two beautiful granddaughters and one adorable grandson. He is an avid runner and has completed over 40 marathons as well as numerous other distance races.

Brian McNulty is a Senior Professional Development Associate for The Leadership and Learning Center. Brian brings 30 years of experience in leadership development as a nationally recognized educator to his current position at The Center. Previously he served as the Vice President for Field Services at Mid-continent Research for Education and Learning (McREL) and was an Assistant Superintendent for Adams County School District 14 and the Assistant Commissioner of Education for the Colorado Department of Education.

Brian's work and writing have been featured in books, scholarly journals, and periodicals throughout the world. An author of more than 40 publications, Brian's most recent books include *Leaders Make It Happen* with Laura Besser (an American Association of School Administrators member book) and *School Leadership that Works: From Research to Results*, an ASCD best-selling publication coauthored with Robert Marzano and Timothy Waters.

Although Brian is well known as both a researcher and a keynote speaker, his primary work has focused on long-term intensive partnerships with schools, districts, state education agencies, and educational service agencies in applying the current research to field-based problems. His recent research has focused on developing continuous improvement frameworks based on data and inquiry.

Linda Gregg is a Senior Professional Development Associate with The Leadership and Learning Center. She is also the Director of Education for a residential treatment center in New Mexico. Linda is the author of *Response to Instructional Strategies and Interventions: Scenarios for K–12 Educators* (2012) and "Crossing the Canyon: Helping Students with Special Needs Achieve," a chapter in *Ahead of the Curve: The Power of Assessment to Transform Teaching and Learning* (2007). Linda is also the author of "RTI Meets Data Teams," a chapter in *Data Teams: The Big Picture*, and The Leadership and Learning Center's "Power Strategies for Response to Intervention" seminar.

Linda holds professional credentials in general education, special education, and school administration. She has taught elementary through high school and has served as an elementary and high school principal. She is a former Associate Superintendent of Federal Programs and Assistant Professor and Coordinator of the Special Education Program at the College of Santa Fe in New Mexico.

Linda is recognized for her expertise in working with diverse learners and bridging the achievement gap for students with special education needs. She is a regional, national, and international speaker as well as a leadership performance coach. Linda has conducted numerous interactive, hands-on seminars on a variety of subjects, including *Data Teams, Decision Making for Results, Power Strategies for Effective Teaching, "Unwrapping" the Standards, Engaging Classroom Assessments, Common Formative Assessments*, and *Effective Implementation of Response to Instructional Intervention.*

Chris Weber is a Professional Development Associate with The Leadership and Learning Center. He is a consultant and administrative coach. He delivers trainings and presentations on Pyramid Response to Intervention, an approach to RTI centered on Professional Learning Communities at Work™ concepts and strategies. Chris also specializes in behavior interventions and addressing behavioral needs as an essential component to each child's academic success.

As principal of R.H. Dana Elementary School in the Capistrano Unified School District in California, Chris was the leader of a highly effective professional learning community. Designated school-wide Title I, with more than 60 percent of all students being English language learners and Latino and more than 75 percent socioeconomically disadvantaged, R.H. Dana consistently exceeded adequate yearly progress (AYP) goals. The school's gains over four years were among the top one percent in the state, and it was the first school in the decades-long history of the Capistrano Unified School District to win the State of California's Title I Academic Achievement Award. Under his leadership, R.H. Dana earned the first California Distinguished School Award in the school's 42-year history. After the percentage of students meeting AYP in English and math tripled in four years, the school was named a National Blue Ribbon School. Chris credits these achievements to the daily practice of key principles: focusing on student engagement, maximizing instructional time, reallocating resources, and developing systematic student support programs based on RTI.

Chris has taught grades K–12 and served as a site administrator for elementary and secondary schools. He was Director of Instruction for the Garden Grove Unified School District in California, which was the 2004 winner of the prestigious Broad Prize for Urban Education. During this time, all groups of students in the district's 47 K–6 schools achieved double-digit AYP gains in mathematics and English language arts.

Chris earned his master's degree from California State University, San Marcos, and his doctorate from the University of California (Irvine and Los Angeles). He is a graduate of the United States Air Force Academy and a former U.S. Air Force pilot.

Lillian A. Hawkins is a Senior Professional Development Associate with The Leadership and Learning Center. Currently, she is the Vice President of the Princeton City School District Board of Education, located near Cincinnati, Ohio. Lillian offers more than 30 years of experience as an educator and principal. She has facilitated school improvement teams, strategic planning, and assessment development; worked as an administrative substitute at all levels K–12; conducted diversity training; facilitated community focus groups; coached and mentored new principals; served as a PRAXIS III assessor for entry-year teachers in the state of Ohio; and taught as an adjunct professor at Miami University in Oxford, Ohio.

Lillian is passionate about working with teachers and leaders to improve student achievement. She believes that every child can learn and that every teacher, as the content expert, is best equipped to tap into that child's hidden resources. Lillian's own inner child is alive and well and available for consultation. As a People to People Student Ambassador Delegation Leader, Lillian traveled the world with students for 10 years, visiting Australia, New Zealand, England, Ireland, Scotland, Wales, France, Germany, Switzerland, Italy, and Greece. She is also a certified lay speaker for the United Methodist Church, and in her free time continues to travel the world, play golf, read, and write.

Lillian earned her bachelor's degree from Wichita State University, her master's degree from the University of Cincinnati, her administrative certifications as principal and assistant superintendent from Xavier University in Cincinnati, and her superintendent license from Miami University, in Oxford, Ohio. Lillian completed her Ph.D. in Educational Administration in the department of Educational Leadership at Miami University, Oxford, Ohio.

Polly Patrick is a Professional Development Associate for The Leadership and Learning Center. She consults with schools to help teachers reach their potential in working with students to improve their potential. Every successful person has at least one teacher they point to who has had a profound positive impact on their lives; Polly wants to develop those teachers.

Currently, Polly splits her time between being a classroom teacher and serving as a Teacher Instructional Coach for the Minnetonka Public Schools in Minnetonka, Minnesota. She also is an Adjunct Instructor at the University of St. Thomas and a consultant focusing on instructional strategies that lead to success, brain-based learning, and professional development that enables educators to work collaboratively to create effective schools.

As a committed life-long learner, Polly has studied the many facets of learning theory and their connections with instructional strategies and teacher behaviors that enable students to achieve. As a voracious reader, Polly enjoys gathering the expertise and perspective of researchers and practitioners, because she believes we are all reaching for the same goal of transforming classrooms and entire schools to best help students achieve.

Polly has intentionally stayed in the classroom with high school students throughout her career. For most of her career she has chosen to also work in higher education with both pre-service and veteran teachers, to support professional development with teachers as a coach in their classrooms, and to work as a consultant in more formal workshops. More recently, Polly has also served as a Staff Development Specialist for new teachers. In all of these venues, the goal is to help teachers be most effective in understanding and leading in the learning process.

In the last five years, Polly has been involved in the Instructional Leadership Team and the Grading and Reporting Committee that have been at the core of creating a learning culture at Minnetonka High School. Polly has traveled to multiple districts and national conferences promoting the value of creating grading systems that give an accurate reflection of what students know and can do.

In her free time, Polly enjoys time with her husband, grown children, and friends. She enjoys summer walks, concerts in the park, time spent on the shore of Lake Superior, and serving as a leader in her church.

Deborah M. Telfer is Director of the University of Dayton's School of Education and Health Sciences Grant Center in Dublin, Ohio. She serves as principal investigator/project director of several federally funded initiatives, including the National Center on Educational Outcomes (NCEO) technical assistance and dissemination effort called Moving Your Numbers. As part of this work, she authored several publications, including *Moving Your Numbers: Five Districts Share How They Used Assessment and Accountability to Increase Performance for Students with Disabilities as Part of District-wide Improvement.*

A school psychologist by training, Deborah held a variety of leadership roles during her 23-year tenure at the Ohio Department of Education (ODE), including serving as associate and interim director of ODE's Office for Exceptional Children, and executive director of the department's Center for School Improvement. In these roles, she supported the initiation of the Ohio Leadership Advisory Council and the Ohio Improvement Process, developed and oversaw implementation of Ohio's State Personnel Development Grant, and coordinated the development and growth of Ohio's statewide system of support in partnership with other ODE offices and Ohio's regional network of state support teams and educational service centers.

Deborah earned her bachelor's, master's, and doctorate degrees from The Ohio State University in the areas of psychology, school psychology, and special education leadership and administration. Her work is primarily focused on systems design and partnership models to support the continuous and sustainable improvement of learning outcomes for all students, particularly students with disabilities and other marginalized groups of students.

Mary Piper is a Professional Development Associate with The Leadership and Learning Center. She has worked for more than 35 years in public education, most recently serving as the Associate Superintendent for Curriculum and Instruction for the Hazelwood School District. She also served one year as the interim superintendent for the district. Prior to becoming the Associate Superintendent in 2008, Dr. Piper served two years as the Assistant Superintendent for Curriculum and Professional Development and five years as an elementary school principal.

Prior to working with The Leadership and Learning Center, Dr. Piper was a client of The Center, which resulted in her being a certified trainer for a large urban school district.

Mary holds a doctorate in educational administration and a master's degree in teaching from St. Louis University. She has a bachelor's degree from Fontbonne University in education/special education. Her post-doctoral work was completed at the University of Virginia's School Turnaround Specialist Program, a joint venture of the Darden School of Business and the Curry School of Education.

Mary especially enjoys working with practitioners in large urban and small rural school districts and putting her extensive K–12 experience to use. She, her husband, and their daughters enjoy spending time with their large extended family, reading, traveling, and watching the St. Louis Cardinals. The Piper family also includes two adopted dogs: a dachshund and a chiweenie. Each day in the Piper household is truly a wonderful new adventure.

Angela Peery is a Senior Professional Development Associate for The Leadership and Learning Center. Previously she was a Teacher Specialist with the South Carolina Department of Education and worked with a chronically low-performing middle school as part of a turnaround team. Angela was also a consultant for the National Urban Alliance for Effective Education.

Angela's experience includes classroom teaching, high school administration, and various leadership roles at the building, district, and state levels. She has taught at both the undergraduate and graduate levels on campus and online. She was also a codirector of a National Writing Project site in South Carolina for several years.

A Virginia native, Angela earned her bachelor's degree in English at Randolph-Macon Woman's College and her master's degree in liberal arts at Hollins College. She is certified in secondary English, secondary administration, and gifted/talented education.

Angela earned her doctorate in curriculum through the University of South Carolina in 2000. She has published six books and has another in progress. Angela has created several seminars for The Center, including the *Writing to Learn* series, *Power Strategies for Effective Teaching*, *Core Literacy*, and *Understanding and Teaching Argumentative Writing*. She is a featured presenter at many of The Center's conferences, summits, and institutes and works both nationally and internationally.

Her family consists of her husband, Tim, two Labrador retrievers, and a cat. They live in the coastal area of Beaufort/Hilton Head in South Carolina and can often be found boating in the local waters or entertaining friends at home.

Introduction

Angela Peery

The Common Core State Standards are now a reality in most states in our nation, and educators are grappling with the implications as they wait for new high-stakes assessments to take effect. As with any curricular or instructional change, educators have concerns about implementing these new standards. Chief among those concerns is the worry that struggling students will struggle even more mightily in the Common Core era.

This handbook has been developed to help teachers and administrators reflect upon the needs of students who struggle with being academically successful. Whether those struggles are related to poverty, language acquisition, ineffective feedback, reluctance to engage, or a host of other reasons, support can be found in the following pages. This handbook is intended to be practical, offering multiple and flexible examples for educators to take away and adapt to their unique situations. The underlying premise of this volume is that all students can find success when being instructed well—even in the age of the new, more rigorous Common Core standards.

In Chapter One, "Boosting Background Knowledge for All Students," author Lillian Hawkins reminds us of the important role that prior knowledge plays in the learning process. She addresses the links among background knowledge, literacy, and poverty and describes concrete actions that can be taken at both the school and classroom levels. Hawkins provides doable advice that will help build background knowledge for a wide variety of students, including English language learners, special education students, and students who struggle yet defy a label.

Polly Patrick focuses on teacher feedback in Chapter Two, "Feedback: Fuel for Learning." John Hattie and numerous other researchers have studied the power of feedback in the last decade and have all come to the same conclusion: effective feedback is absolutely necessary in order for students to learn at high levels. Patrick explores not only what effective feedback is, but also why it is even more critical as we begin to teach to the Common Core expectations. She also discusses mindset as a critical component of students' ability to receive and use feedback as they learn to self-monitor. This chapter is a must-read as we all begin to reflect on our teaching methods and refine our interactions with students as we support them in reaching proficiency in these new, higher standards.

Chapter Three discusses the all-important instructional concept of scaffolding learning. Author Linda Gregg provides a clear, eight-step sequence that teachers can use to ensure that effective scaffolding occurs. She then expertly illustrates the recommended process through two authentic, classroom-based examples. Within the examples are descriptions of many research-proven, effective strategies. Every educator should easily find food for thought in this chapter, whether it's the reminder of a strategy that hasn't been employed in a while, or steps in the scaffolding sequence that could be better executed.

In Chapter Four, "Building Vocabulary Knowledge So All Students Can Tell Stories," Mary Piper addresses the crucial topic of vocabulary acquisition and use, which has come into sharper focus because of the Common Core English language arts standards' emphasis on it. Piper succinctly presents the most salient research on vocabulary instruction and then offers concrete ideas about how educators might select exactly which words are most important to teach. The recommendations of several experts in vocabulary instruction are then summarized, and the chapter ends with specific information applicable to struggling students. Teachers of all grade levels and subjects should be prompted to reflect on the current state of vocabulary instruction in their classrooms as they read this provocative chapter.

Chapter Five focuses specifically on secondary school students and how effective differentiation can be achieved. Thomas Hierck addresses the unique challenges that secondary school teachers face and offers differentiation as a concept that will assist them in raising academic achievement dramatically. Connections among differentiation, mastery learning, direct instruction, and Response to Intervention (RTI) are drawn. Student behavior, motivation, and engagement are also addressed. As Hierck notes, "Teachers are in the best position to create a differentiated environment that enriches the life of each student. In this environment, students gain the ability to close the gaps in their academic learning and acquire appropriate behaviors." This chapter will help teachers do just that.

Chris Weber's chapter, the penultimate one in this volume, examines effective direct instruction for all learners, but especially in light of the RTI process. He quickly takes us through a review of several models of effective instruction and then turns our attention to the necessary components of a good lesson or series of lessons. These components remain unchanged from the past but are perhaps now more deserving of our attention than ever as we seek to teach to the demands of the Common Core. Specific templates are offered to guide educators with thinking and planning. As the author says, "the best intervention is prevention," and with properly executed direct instruction, many struggling students can surely find increased success.

The last chapter differs from the others in the book, as it focuses on a specific research project called Moving Your Numbers. This project studied demographically different school districts from across the country that were using assessment and accountability measures to improve performance for all students in their districts. Coauthors Brian McNulty and Deb Telfer explain the core practices and underlying assumptions that guided the work of these districts and include abundant examples about how the work was carried out. The chapter resoundingly demonstrates that success is possible with all students—those identified for special education, English language learners, and others that need extensive support for various reasons.

Navigating Achievement for Struggling Students with the Common Core State Standards, the fifth book in The Leadership and Learning Center's *Getting Ready for the Common Core Handbook Series,* provides multiple views on a very complex subject—what to do to better serve struggling students as we embrace the Common Core State Standards. Through the different voices, experiences, and counsel here, we hope that you find support (and a new nugget of wisdom or two) for the hard work that you do in the world of education. Enjoy.

CHAPTER ONE

Boosting Background Knowledge for All Students

Lillian A. Hawkins

Ready or not, students come to school. Teachers find within a single classroom many varied levels of student preparedness based on culture, socioeconomic factors, and gaps in academic achievement. And yet, it is the educational goal of the teacher to take students from wherever they are when they come, to a level of proficiency as exemplified by the Common Core State Standards (CCSS). Although the CCSS provide a destination for instruction, they do not equip teachers with a process for getting there. Teachers, equipped with the knowledge of their students' unique learning needs and proven best practices, will forge a way to greater achievement.

DEFINING BACKGROUND KNOWLEDGE

The terms "background knowledge" and "prior knowledge" are often used interchangeably. Background knowledge is what students already know before they step into the classroom. It is the sum of their experiences outside the classroom, and the platform upon which teachers build new learning and connect it to previous learning. Background knowledge includes what students already know about particular content, their personal knowledge about strategies and procedures, and their self-knowledge. Robert Marzano says that one of the features of background knowledge is that it is stored in what can be thought of as "packets" of information or "memory records." Understanding these memory records gives clear guidance for enhancing or boosting academic background knowledge (Marzano, 2004). Background knowledge manifests itself in vocabulary knowledge.

WHY IS BACKGROUND KNOWLEDGE IMPORTANT?

Students learn best when they can connect new information to previous concepts, vocabulary, strategies, and activities from earlier learning experiences. Background knowledge is stored in permanent memory. When students come from a number of different feeder schools, not to mention different school districts, states, and countries, it's sometimes difficult for the teacher to know where to begin a lesson.

What students already know is one of the strongest indicators of how well they will learn new information (Marzano, 2004). If the knowledge and skills that students from advantaged backgrounds possess is learned rather than innate, then students who do not come from advantaged backgrounds can learn it, too. Indeed, even aspects of intelligence once thought to be genetically based appear to be amenable to change through schooling. To accomplish such a task, schools must be willing to dedicate the necessary time and resources to enhancing the academic background knowledge of students, particularly those who do not come from affluent backgrounds.

Academic vocabulary and concepts learned in another language are just as valid as those learned in English, but school curriculum in other countries may have a different focus.

English as a second language (ESL) lesson plans require building background knowledge support within ESL activities and core lessons, especially for such subjects as American history and American culture. Creating a common ground upon which to build new learning equalizes student background knowledge as much as possible. Teachers working with ESL students within the context of a diverse classroom with multiple cultural identities also must deal with very different social norms. It is important for teachers to assess the background knowledge of each of their students before moving to instruction.

Marzano (2004) says that background knowledge manifests itself as vocabulary knowledge. The key is providing students who do not have vocabulary-rich environments with opportunities to learn and experience a wider base of vocabulary that can be linked to previous and new learning. Marzano's research indicates that "...what students already know about the content is one of the strongest indicators of how well they will learn new information" (p. 30). Therefore, it is critical that teachers spend more time with focused instruction to build background knowledge. While different kinds of background knowledge can be important to students, depending on their interests and the nonacademic areas of their lives, it is academic background knowledge that most affects a future tied to academic achievement.

LITERACY

Literacy is the foundation of academic success. That, coupled with background knowledge, lays the framework for achievement. Gaps in achievement occur when students struggle with the content because of their varied entry levels of performance. Some households are full of books and contain parents who read to their children and who model reading. Other households are devoid of books and magazines, and even conversation. Consequently, students do not learn how to talk about their environment, or how to delineate processes and procedures. Kristina Robertson (2007) says that the efforts that teachers make to add a rich, cultural dimension to the curriculum will add dimension to students' understanding as they connect with literature on three levels: text to text, text to self, and self to world. Students' home literacy environments may never have included interactions on these three levels.

Children need literacy skills to be successful in school. Previous classroom and state assessments have shown that school success depends upon high literacy and math abilities. Family literacy programs, such as the Success For All reading program (www. successforall.org), put books into every home and require that students read to an adult at home. The Success for All program has been found to increase reading achievement; cut the achievement gap between African-American, Hispanic, and white students; and prepare teachers to support the needs of English language learners. In order to successfully connect with parents, family literacy programs need to be respectful of parents and sensitive to cultural differences. Parents should also be included in the planning and development to ensure success at school (Hiatt-Michael, 2001).

Eric Hirsch (2006) says that reading proficiency is at the very heart of the democratic educational enterprise as conceived by Thomas Jefferson, with the ideal being to offer *all* children the opportunity to succeed, regardless of who their parents happen to be. Hirsch goes on to say that schools have failed to live up to the basic ideal of a democratic education. The good news is that the academic achievement gaps among social groups can be narrowed with literacy instruction. Richard Allington (2002) would profess that the teacher is the heart of literacy success. "Good teachers, effective teachers, manage to produce better achievement regardless of which curriculum materials, pedagogical approach, or reading program is selected" (p. 1). When parents and great teachers work together to focus on and support literacy instruction and to utilize background knowledge as they together create new experiences for students, then achievement is a certainty. This creates the supportive conversational environment that sustains reading, increases motivation, and deepens understanding.

Douglas Reeves' (2004) research on 90/90/90 schools has shown that progress can be made and achievement gaps can be narrowed with the appropriate application of interventions despite the relationship among poverty, ethnicity, and academic achievement. The characteristics of 90/90/90 schools are that more than 90 percent of the students are eligible for free or reduced lunch, more than 90 percent are ethnic minorities, and more than 90 percent met or achieved high academic standards in reading or another subject on their state tests of achievement. Academic achievement is highly prized in 90/90/90 schools. Part of what must be taught to students whose background knowledge needs to be increased is to value academic success and to put an emphasis on writing, because increased nonfiction writing has a significant impact on students' test scores in all disciplines.

Literacy frees students to see a world beyond the walls of their homes and their schools. The basic tenet of education is to bring all children to a common place.

POVERTY

Generational poverty (poverty that has plagued a family for several generations) and situational poverty (poverty that has come about due to a sudden change of circumstances, such as job loss, homelessness, or medical expenses), as described by Ruby Payne (1998), are no longer excuses for not helping students to achieve. Poverty negatively influences access to academically oriented experiences. Poor children do not have opportunities for books in the home or social and cultural experiences outside the home such as museums, entertainment, travel, restaurants, and so on, that afford a richer base of interactions with the world at large.

The relationship between poverty and ethnicity negatively compounds the impact on academic achievement for black and Hispanic children when compared to white children (Marzano, 2004). Katherine Jones (2007) concurs that childhood poverty correlates with poor academic performance, lower IQ scores, and higher dropout rates. She further reports that the longer children live in poverty, the lower their level of academic achievement. Building conceptual frameworks and cognitive strategies in language instruction builds literacy and increases background knowledge and thus boosts achievement. Schools must take responsibility for providing experiences, resources, materials, and even personal attention to make up for the deficits at home. This can be achieved through programs that support schools, such as adult volunteers, tutorial assistance, off-site and virtual field trips, and donations from business partners that include time and money. Eli Johnson and Michelle Karns (2011) say teachers are eagerly looking for strategies to improve the learning experience for challenged students. They assert that the children most in need of instructional intervention strategies are:

1. Children raised in poverty, those living in chaos, and those living without adult models.

2. Children who are English language learners.

3. Children who struggle with phonological processing, memory difficulties, and speech or hearing impairments.

Because these students lack the resources in their homes to give them the background knowledge that would better prepare them for school, the school must intervene to keep them from falling behind their peers or dropping out of school.

BEST PRACTICES: WHAT THE SCHOOL CAN DO

Schools can provide academically enriching experiences, especially for students whose home lives do not do so naturally, through a direct approach (Marzano, 2004). Such direct experiences would include field trips to museums and art galleries, theater excursions, and school-sponsored travel and exchange programs. Although such programs would be unquestionably beneficial and enriching, they are not always fiscally feasible. This is where school partnerships can be beneficial. District leadership and/or parent/teacher organizations can forge relationships with local and corporate businesses to provide financial support and physical support in the way of volunteers to work with children at school or in their work environs. Even providing transportation for field trips is a tremendous boost for schools in creating learning opportunities for all kids.

In addition to the direct approach of field trips, Marzano also suggests mentoring relationships where students pair one-to-one with a caring adult, and indirect approaches where experiences that build background knowledge are created for students within the school day. Direct experience has always been one strategy for enhancing students' knowledge. Field trips, hands-on learning experiments, and exposure were the tools for providing students with direct and personal knowledge of new facts or events. Schools today are limited by financial and scheduling constraints, so sometimes alternative experiences must be provided instead of direct experiences. This is another opportunity for school and business partnerships to tackle an important educational need.

Marzano (2004) maintains that implementation of the six principles for building an indirect approach will enhance students' background knowledge even without direct experiences such as field trips or mentoring relationships. Schools that use indirect approaches in vocabulary and reading and language instruction should ensure their programs have the following characteristics:

- They have the goal of installing background knowledge in permanent memory. This means that all children will know and understand certain experiences so that those experiences are always available for activation, even without awareness.

- They ensure students have multiple exposures to target information to facilitate storage in permanent memory. This means students have multiple opportunities to convert an experience to permanent memory, so that it becomes a part of them and part of their working memory.

- They focus on the development of surface-level but accurate knowledge across a broad spectrum of subject areas. This means that domain-specific vocabulary is critical and is targeted in every discipline. Vocabulary instruction is not reserved for English language arts only.

- The instructional techniques focus on the linguistic and nonlinguistic aspects of background knowledge. This means that teachers use nonlinguistic representations like graphic organizers and kinesthetic activity, among other methods, to activate and increase background knowledge. Teachers must be skilled in using the various forms of nonlinguistic representation and must use them frequently.

- They focus on developing labels for packets of experiential knowledge in the tradition of direct vocabulary instruction. This gives students the opportunity to represent what they learn in new ways, using new words for new experiences.

- They rely on the generation of virtual experiences in working memory through wide reading, language interaction, and educational visual media. This means schools have a wide variety of options for providing students with sensory and visual experiences that can move from working memory to permanent memory.

School leaders can also make sure that teachers provide effective instruction. Another factor in building background knowledge is teacher talent. John Hattie (2009) says that teachers are among the most powerful influences on learning. Great teachers get great results, no matter what the challenge. Hattie submits that teachers can typically attain an increase in effect size, a measure of outcome variables, of between 0.20 and 0.40 over the course of one school year. This is a very powerful influence on a student's academic achievement. Hattie's research has shown that variance in teacher effectiveness accounts for a significant percentage of the variance in student achievement. Cathy Lassiter (2012) urges that school leaders work to deliberately develop teacher talent through meaningful feedback and deliberate practice within the school improvement plan. Cheryl Dunkle (2012) reiterates that good teaching, knowing your learners, knowing your content, and knowing instructional strategies will improve instruction and raise student achievement. Specific best practices are discussed in greater detail in the next section.

School leaders can connect to parents and to the community. Diana Hiatt-Michael (2001) stresses the importance of parent involvement in connecting schools to families and to communities. Such partnerships would enhance learning at home, enabling teachers to help parents by partnering with them in delivering instruction to students. Families could be involved with interactive homework, academic and career goal setting, and participating in literacy projects. Good partnerships and shared responsibilities illustrate the "it takes a village to raise a child" philosophy. Connecting with community resources allows students to be exposed to 21st-century skills in a more fiscally sound manner and ties into real-life experiences. Families and schools working together to promote the best interest of the students can only increase academic achievement.

BEST PRACTICES: WHAT THE TEACHER CAN DO

There are many instructional strategies that a general education teacher might utilize to address the needs of diverse learners, especially those with diverse backgrounds and diverse abilities. Here are some activities that will help teachers to assess and home in on students' background knowledge:

- Ask open-ended questions:
  - How many of you have ever...?
  - When have you...?
  - Tell about a time when you felt...?

- Have students do a "quick-write" to reveal connections to a scientific process, a historical situation, or a literary theme.

- Have students draw or artistically depict how they could connect their reading to their own life experience.

- Use intervention strategies on a daily basis to improve reading, listening, numeracy, speaking, and writing.

- Make connections to your students' families to broaden their academic connections.

One way to remediate academic gaps in learning for students who do not have sufficient background knowledge is through intervention. Response to Intervention (RTI) is a framework that guides instruction for all students. Linda Gregg (2012) describes

RTI as a multi-tiered approach that provides services and interventions at increasing levels of intensity to students who require supplemental learning. The RTI process has the potential to limit academic failure. Teachers can address the needs and gaps in all students at all levels. The entire student population falls within one of three instructional Tiers. Tier 1 represents the high-quality core instruction that all students get. Tier 2 students receive strategic interventions that are directed towards targeted students in the middle tier, usually 10–15 percent of students based on specific instructional needs. Tier 3 represents students in need of intensive intervention, or 1–5 percent of the total student population (Gregg, 2012). For students whose learning problems are related to cultural differences, RTI can limit failure and reduce the number of students who are identified as having learning disabilities.

Effective interventions need to be engaging and use all of the senses. This is especially true for students from poverty. Great intervention strategies are: *engaging,* so that students become intrinsically motivated; *interactive,* to permit collaboration and connection with fellow classmates; and *energizing,* to help students maintain focus as they accelerate their learning (Johnson and Karns, 2011). Using these strategies produces instruction that is highly effective. Struggling students benefit from classroom intervention strategies that (Johnson and Karns, 2011):

- Include explicit, well-organized (systematic) instruction as well as opportunities to read connected text.
- Are provided in small-group or one-on-one formats.
- Provide for 20–40 minutes three to five times per week.

- Provide extended opportunities for practice, including guided, independent, and cumulative practice with teacher feedback.
- Are provided in addition to regular classroom reading instruction.
- Include continuous progress monitoring.

Johnson and Karns go on to say that the core intervention competencies of good instruction are: listening, reading, numeracy, speaking, and writing. These competencies are the heart of the Common Core State Standards. As teachers prepare for implementation of the Common Core, they must also prepare their students for the next generation assessments. Test-taking skills are just as important as content knowledge. Background knowledge is important to level the academic playing field and boost achievement for all students.

SUMMARY

Schools are challenged with more and more students who are academically unprepared to meet the standards of instruction. As we prepare students for a college- and career-ready curriculum and the next generation assessments, it is imperative as part of that preparation that students have background knowledge that will afford them the opportunity to embrace all of the new educational content and experiences, rather than struggling with them. Teachers can attempt to build background knowledge through a direct approach, through mentoring relationships, or through an indirect approach of academic interventions utilizing

RTI. Effective classroom interventions will help students to meet their core intervention competencies: listening, reading, numeracy, speaking, and writing. Effective interventions utilize the six principles of the indirect approach to help students process and store information into permanent memory. Therefore, schools and teachers need to keep in mind and focus on the following:

- Students of poverty
- Students who do not have English as their language of learning
- Mentoring relationships
- Academic interventions

References

Allington, R. (2002). *The six Ts of effective elementary literacy instruction.* Retrieved from http://www.readingrockets.org/article/96/

Dunkle, C. A. (2012). *Leading the common core state standards: From common sense to common practice.* Thousand Oak, CA: Corwin.

Gregg, L. A. (2012). *Response to instructional strategies and interventions: Scenarios for K–12 educators.* Englewood, CO: Lead + Learn Press.

Hattie, J. (2009). *Visible learning: A synthesis of over 800 meta-analyses relating to achievement.* New York, NY: Routledge.

Hiatt-Michael, D. B. (2001). *Promising practices for family involvement in schools.* Greenwich, CT: Information Age Publishing.

Hirsch, Jr., E. D. (2004). *What your fourth grader needs to know: Fundamentals of a good fourth-grade education.* New York, NY: Doubleday.

Hirsch, Jr., E. D. (2006). *The knowledge deficit: Closing the shocking education gap for American children.* Boston: Houghton Mifflin.

Johnson, E., & Karns, M. (2011). *RTI strategies that work in the K–2 classroom.* Larchmont, NY: Eye on Education.

Jones, K. (2007). *Poverty's effect on childhood academic achievement.* Retrieved from voices.yahoo.com/povertys-effect-childhood -academic-achievement-524117.html?cat=4

Lassiter, C. J. (2012). *The secrets and simple truths of high-performing school cultures.* Englewood, CO: Lead + Learn Press.

Marzano, R. J. (2004). *Building background knowledge for academic achievement: Research on what works in schools.* Alexandria, VA: ASCD.

Payne, R. K. (1998). *A framework for understanding poverty.* Baytown, TX: RFT Publishing.

Reeves, D. B. (2004). *Accountability in action: A blueprint for learning organizations* (2nd ed.). Englewood, CO: Lead + Learn Press.

Robertson, K. (2007). *Connect students' background knowledge to content in the ELL classroom.* Retrieved from http://www.readingrockets .org/article/20827/

CHAPTER TWO

Feedback:
Fuel for Learning

Polly Patrick

*"The most powerful form of learning, the most
sophisticated form of staff development, comes not
from listening to the good works of others, but from
sharing what we know with others.... By reflecting
on what we do, by giving it coherence, and by
sharing and articulating our craft knowledge, we
make meaning, we learn."*
—Roland Barth, 1990, p. 120

This chapter is written in the spirit of the above Roland Barth
quote. It was in that same spirit that many of us became educators.
Having interacted with countless educators, I am pleased to share
what I have learned from them and from working with many
struggling students. In addition to my own experience, I share the
wisdom of other authors, all of whom have proven to be great resources to guide educators in our relationships with our students.
I hope that the content presented here will stimulate conversations
with colleagues around this work. The goal is to re-evaluate how
we currently offer feedback and to refocus our energy as we partner with our students to enable them to succeed in CCSS work.

Our first step in providing effective feedback is to understand the challenge. Feedback is "the transmission of evaluative or corrective information about an action, event, or process to the original or controlling source" (www.merriam-webster.com/dictionary/feedback). The definition reminds us that effective feedback is multidimensional. We leave the process too open to misinterpretation if students' feedback consists of a paper returned that merely has a grade on it. What leads us to believe that students benefit from such a message? With as much time as students spend in school, many students understand "doing school" better than they understand authentic learning. We work with struggling students who may have internalized messages to stay very quiet or to act out vociferously to keep the focus away from them, and thus away from what it takes for them to actually learn. We must help students understand that making mistakes actually helps them to create new thinking patterns; then they will come to replicate their efforts on future challenging problems.

We empower students as we teach them the language of learning, and they begin to see results. Douglas Reeves (2011) has said, "If we expect students to improve, then they must take risks, make mistakes, and receive formative feedback that leads to improved performance. . . . If we expect teachers and leaders to improve, then we must provide monitoring and feedback that meet the same criteria" (p.12). The Common Core is designed to ensure that students remain focused on the essential work that is critical for achieving success. We must help students learn persistence when working on fundamental tasks until they "get it," we must offer effective feedback that gives them the map to "learn it," and we must ask guiding questions that help them reflect on how they "got it." Then, and only then, can they replicate the same process the next time they are learning new content or solving challenging problems. Sometimes we too learn the very lesson that we will pass on to them by making our own mistakes.

The Common Core State Standards for mathematics consist of eight mathematical practices that are to be incorporated at every grade level. The very first mathematical practice listed is: "Make sense of problems and persevere in solving them" (CCSSI, 2010). Proficient math students have learned to monitor their thinking and evaluate their process as they work through a difficult math problem. They know both when something isn't working, and when to try another entry point or method to tackle the problem. They understand they might have to try many different ways to figure out a solution. Beyond that, there could be more than one right approach, or even more than one right answer. As teachers, we know all our math students (or students in any subject area) do not automatically have this mentality. We must teach it. But how? Through feedback. If teachers want their students to persevere, teachers must break down the steps of a problem or task, stopping often to give timely, specific, targeted feedback. In this way we encourage students to continue striving to reach proficiency.

TEACHERS, ARE WE LISTENING?

I recall the first day of school one year waiting for 35 students to arrive for my fourth-hour psychology class. I steeled myself for this class because of the five Individualized Education Programs (IEPs) on my desk; one student was legally blind and four were English language learners who would be joining 30 other students of varied interests and abilities. I offered my best attempt at giving them the expectations for the class and an overview of the content as I passed out pages of materials. After the bell rang, there was a quick mass exodus to lunch—except for one young woman. She held out all the papers I had given the class, gave me a bewildered look, and asked in very broken English, "Anything important?" My attempt at reassurance was in the form of a measured reply: "No, come tomorrow and we'll get started again." I fell into my chair.

Little did I realize in those moments that I was learning a valuable lesson about feedback. That student was giving me feedback that I needed. I had moved forward with my plan before knowing what my students needed. We needed to learn about each other, and about the learning process itself, before diving into the course structure and rules, and especially before receiving mounds of materials and content. This young woman changed forever how I start classes.

Are we listening and watching for the feedback our students give us? To seek and "know thy impact" changes our own practice (Hattie, 2012). We do this by inviting feedback from students and using their feedback about how they are learning from us. Their perception of working with us is filtered through their own story. It often differs from how we see ourselves working with them. When those two perceptions merge, the real power of change is released.

I also believe that we can only give away what we have. The extent to which we are effective at inviting, receiving, and using feedback from our students mirrors the extent to which they will become able to invite, receive, and use the feedback that we give them.

INVITING FEEDBACK

I first learned that all "learning is by invitation" from Parker Palmer, the author of works such as *Courage to Teach* (2007). While so much of current education involves preparing students for mandated testing, it's challenging to keep hospitality and invitation alive in the classroom. John Hattie (2012) informs us that the teacher-student relationship is critical for student learning and achievement; it has an effect size of 0.72, which puts it in the top 12 influences on student achievement. Building teacher-student relationships goes way beyond watching or talking about that week's sports events; it also depends on believing that the students can do more than they thought they could while learning in the classroom. I am often asked to help raise the self-esteem of my students; the image of a self-esteem filling station comes to mind. But contrary to that image, it is helping students try something that they believe is too hard and then guiding them to achieve it anyway that truly builds their self-esteem.

Many struggling learners with whom I've worked have a common refrain. There are variations on the theme, but it goes something like, "I just don't get this." Inside these words are learned attitudes and behaviors that hinder students' learning potential. Some students have learned that if they say these words, then some well-meaning adult might do more than just help—that person might essentially do their assignment for them. But in the process, the student's understanding about the concept is often left behind. The first step toward addressing this refrain is using a short questionnaire to discover what the student's current mindset is. The questions in Exhibit 2.1, which was adapted from *Mindset* (2006) by Carol Dweck, can help students (and teachers) discern what their own mindsets are currently.

BOOK
FIVE
**EXHIBIT
2.1**   **Mindset Questionnaire**

MINDSET QUESTIONNAIRE
Choose a number from 0–10, with 10 being the highest.

1. When something disappointing happens to me I'm learning to focus on what actions I can take to make things better.

0	1	2	3	4	5	6	7	8	9	10

2. I may not have started out naturally successful, but I'm learning that when I apply myself I can consistently learn—improving my weaker areas and enhancing my stronger areas.

0	1	2	3	4	5	6	7	8	9	10

3. No matter what my level of intelligence I can always work to change and experience significant improvement.

0	1	2	3	4	5	6	7	8	9	10

4. I enjoy the challenge of learning things that are difficult for me.

0	1	2	3	4	5	6	7	8	9	10

5. Learning is a priority for me; I always pay close attention to information that can increase my knowledge.

0	1	2	3	4	5	6	7	8	9	10

6. I feel most alive when I'm facing challenges.

0	1	2	3	4	5	6	7	8	9	10

7. In any activity I like to "play up"—competing with people who are better than I am currently. This is how I improve my game.

0	1	2	3	4	5	6	7	8	9	10

8. Two statements often go together for me: "this is hard" and "this is fun."

0	1	2	3	4	5	6	7	8	9	10

9. I actually learn more from my failures than my successes; taking responsibility actually helps me feel stronger.

0	1	2	3	4	5	6	7	8	9	10

10. In my work I experiment constantly with what works ... and fit new things into my overall plan.

0	1	2	3	4	5	6	7	8	9	10

Source: Adapted from Dweck, 2006.

The questionnaire in Exhibit 2.1 is helpful in finding new language to use when speaking with students: The higher one's score, the higher one's "growth" mindset. Knowing a student's mindset helps us discuss with students the mindset that we both bring to the task of learning. Conversation about the questionnaire can also give the teacher new insights into how students approach their work. Exploring the differences between a growth mindset and a fixed mindset gives teachers and students a shared perspective when working through the frustrations inherent in the learning process. Exhibit 2.2 offers a brief overview of the differences between a fixed mindset and a growth mindset.

BOOK FIVE EXHIBIT 2.2 **Fixed Versus Growth Mindset**

Fixed Mindset	Growth Mindset
Trying to look smart	Learning to become smart
Avoiding challenge	Embracing challenge
Giving up easily	Persisting when faced with setbacks
Effort is fruitless	More effort, more mastery
Ignoring negative feedback	Learning from criticism
Threatened by success of others	Inspired by success of others

Source: Adapted from Dweck, 2006.

So, how do we help students shift their mindsets? The first part of developing a growth mindset is requiring that students add one more word when they say "I don't get it"—the word "yet" (Dweck, 2006). The ongoing work in giving feedback to struggling learners starts with language that helps both teachers and students move from attitudes that students are not good learners, which hold them captive, to the freedom of seeing themselves as smarter than they previously thought they were. The relationship between the teacher and the learners is the corner post for this work.

Many struggling learners no longer believe that they can succeed in school. Students may need to draft off a teacher's belief until they believe it for themselves. So, how do we make that happen? This kind of change isn't a one-time thing. When students who had been progressing get stuck again, I pull out the continuum in Exhibit 2.3 and have them point to where they are right now, and then I support them in developing strategies to move forward.

BOOK FIVE EXHIBIT 2.3   **Mindset Continuum**

Enduring   **Enjoying**

FIXED Mindset   Raising my **AWARENESS**   **DECIDING** new direction   **LEARNING** to apply concepts   **GROWTH** Mindset

When students are stuck and the teacher is trying to introduce the student to "new thinking," every part of the continuum in Exhibit 2.3 might sound negative. The goal is to move toward the positive end through conversation. At this point, it really helps if common language about mindsets can be used by as many people as possible who work with the same student. The stages of progress toward a growth mindset are as follows (adapted from Dweck, 2006):

1. Fixed mindset: Never—I can't imagine thinking this way.

2. Awareness: I am realizing it's possible to think this way.

3. Deciding: I want to approach things this way—and I will.

4. Learning: I'm reminding myself regularly and making progress.

5. Growth mindset: This is becoming a more natural response—I'm enjoying it.

Educators can help students begin using new patterns of thinking until it becomes their "new normal." In pedagogical psychology, we call this "overlearning." Costa and Kallick write about overlearning in *Habits of Mind* (2012). Much like the muscle memory that is sought by an athlete, we want new learning memory to be incorporated into a student's thinking. John Hattie reminds us that students have to be able to sustain practice until they "get it": "... Herein lies a major link between challenge and feedback, two of the essential ingredients of learning. The greater the challenge the higher the probability that one seeks and needs feedback, but the more important it is that there is a teacher to provide feedback and to ensure that the learner is on the right path to successfully meet the challenges" (Hattie, 2012, p. 17). The persuasive invitation from the teacher is a signature portion of that feedback. Only by knowing the students' stories can teachers help them learn the necessary commitment.

Students also need to see short-term gains. They need to believe that they can achieve. In her book *How Your Child Learns Best* (2008), Dr. Judith Willis speaks of how learning promotes learning: "The more times one repeats an action (practice) or recalls the information (review), the more dendrites sprout to connect new memories to old ones (plasticity), the stronger the connections between neurons become, and the more efficient the brain becomes at retrieving that memory or repeating the action" (p. 13). The key is to work on the motivation to stay with the learning to see the success. Students sometimes only want to do a task in which they already are proficient. Graham Nuthall, in *The Hidden Lives of Learners* (2007), reminds us that we have to have three to four interactions with content to move it from the working memory to the long-term memory. If that prior knowledge can be attached to the new learning, then the students win.

The invitation to learn has to be based on the students' real belief that they can learn; as teachers, our behavior and words influence that belief greatly. Language that can help shape attitudes and mindsets needs to be in place. Creating a growth mindset can't be accomplished through a checklist or a recipe; it's work that is never done. The teacher's invitation creates the first exchange in a dialogue that features ongoing conversations and a celebration of learning at the end of the students' time in the class. Creating a growth mindset prepares students to be ready to hear realistic, helpful feedback on their progress.

GIVING AND RECEIVING FEEDBACK

Not all feedback is equal. Perhaps you have had the experience of receiving some feedback that was not helpful. Maybe you even received feedback that made you wonder whether or not you should continue with the task. The new edition of *Classroom Instruction That Works* (Dean, Hubbell, Pitler, and Stone, 2012) lists four key characteristics of effective feedback, which are consistent across the abundant research available:

- Addresses what is correct and elaborates on what students need to do next.
- Is appropriately in time to meet students' needs.
- Is criterion-referenced, not norm-referenced.
- Engages students in the feedback process.

Each of these characteristics is critical for struggling learners. Students need to know what they can do to better their thinking and their work. This is in stark contrast to just returning a student paper that has 10 out of 20 facts marked correct. The Common Core documents stress that it no longer is enough to simply know math facts, without knowing how the numbers work in relation to each other. Students will need to learn from our feedback how to ask questions that will enable them to solve the problem. In English language arts, it is not enough to know vocabulary without building meaning. Students will need to draft off us to learn how to think while reading complex text to deepen their understanding. It takes more practice, and more specific feedback, to construct meaning.

How feedback is given and received is also critical. Feedback must be given so that it can be heard. Feedback must be timely and appropriate, and must address a student's needs, but it won't be heard if it overloads the student's capacity to process it. In *Why Don't Students Like School?* (2009), Daniel Willingham states, "Overloads of working memory are caused by such things as multistep instructions, lists of unconnected facts, chains of logic more than two or three steps long, and the application of a just-learned concept to new material" (p. 20). It may seem efficient to give students all the directions we believe they need to finish the task. The key is to give enough feedback for the student to know how to keep moving forward and not so much that they shut down.

Feedback has a critical role in student achievement according to John Hattie (2012). Feedback yields a 0.75 effect size on his measurement scale of 150 factors impacting student achievement. That makes it one of the top 10 influences on that list. Hattie outlines three key questions that need to be at the heart of feedback:

• Where am I going? (goals)

• How am I going there? (performance as measured against goals)

• What next? (future goals)

Conversations build value when they are ongoing and do not just occur at the beginning of the unit. These concepts are not only for struggling students, but also for students who are already strong and doing well. Teachers and students must work together to make sure that the goals are clear and that the students regularly know both how far they have come and how far they have to go.

Hattie (2012) describes four types of feedback: feedback on task, feedback on process, feedback on self-monitoring, and feedback on self. It is important to point out that the first three are the most critical for learning. The types of feedback are summarized in Exhibit 2.4.

Hattie (2012) goes on to describe feedback as "just in time, just for me, just for where I am in my learning process, and just

Types of Feedback

BOOK FIVE
EXHIBIT 2.4

Type of Feedback	Examples of Feedback
Task— Teacher leading to help get students heading in the right direction	Examples of correct/incorrect answers: "Check your work against these..."
Process— Furthering the thinking that they are already doing, but that may need refining	Connections between ideas. Use of hints or clues to help students identify mistakes: "Could you try...?"
Self-monitoring— Student is taking more of the leadership, but teacher is giving guiding questions to help students gain confidence in their thinking.	Enables students to evaluate their own thinking and learning: "What do you think could correct/enhance your thinking here?"
Self— Most potential for being positive or negative; when used as part of the invitation to learn as affirmation of students as learners, this can be very positive.	Negative—general praise Positive—affirmation within a relationship of trust

Source: Adapted from Hattie, 2012.

what I need to help me move forward" (p. 122). I find that giving feedback "just in time" is a great motivator for my students. When they receive timely feedback, students come to know that we are partners in their learning. When the feedback speaks of their work, students know that the teacher knows and cares about them. When the feedback works, they believe that the teacher is aware of their learning process and committed to them moving forward. That is real student-teacher partnership and power.

USING FEEDBACK

Feedback promotes the metacognition (reflection) that enables students to know what they have learned and how they have learned it. Their learning can then be replicated with future concepts and challenges. The press of time often leads teachers to pass over reflection, but this is one of the most critical components of learning. It is not enough that the teacher can articulate the goals or the successes of their students. When students identify and articulate their own progress, they can repeat the process. The students know more about themselves and their learning. Returning to Hattie's rankings of the effectiveness of 150 different factors on student achievement, metacognitive strategies have a 0.69 effect size, making them fourteenth on the influence list (2012). Hattie's research shows that self-monitoring/self-regulation has an effect size of 1.44 on student achievement (2012). This makes it the number one influence. What Hattie's research shows about the effect size of feedback on student achievement is reflected in the Common Core State Standards.

How will we as teachers help students become more reflective during the pace and rigor of the CCSS? The art of asking questions is crucial at this point. Listening to the answers is even more crucial. Teachers must ask questions that focus on student learning and not merely review content material. In *Making Thinking Visible* (2011), Ron Ritchhart, Mark Church, and Karin Morrison refer to these questions as the authentic questions that construct understanding. Teachers become a mirror during this phase, as they encourage students to move ahead in controlling their own learning. I so often hear John Hattie's mantra ringing in my ears: "When teachers *see* learning through the eyes of my students and I help students become their own teachers" (2012, p. 5). Let's look at how the CCSS are designed to have the students do just that.

The CCSS documents describe seven characteristics of students who are college- and career-ready. The first characteristic is that they demonstrate independence. The goal is to take away the external scaffolding so that students become self-directed learners. As was mentioned previously, students will say they "don't get it," and will then "wait out" the teacher, hoping for the answer. Yet part of effective teaching is allowing students to struggle. Struggling students often cannot navigate their own thinking, and this is where patience comes into play. Educators must allow students time to think, and therefore struggle, and at the same time, must be ready to give specific feedback so the students do not stay stuck. The power of students "figuring out" something for themselves is worth the extra time and energy. It empowers and motivates students, and most importantly, changes their thinking to a "can do" attitude. As students become self-directed learners, they learn to seek out information, peer support, and teacher help on their own.

As students think something through, they learn to pay attention to their own thinking. The Common Core demands that students develop better and higher-order thinking skills, so it's vital that teachers start and reinforce metacognition in the classroom. Students learn the attitudes and questions they need to succeed from us, and we can only give away what we have. Therefore, our own practice of verbalizing our own thinking as we are learning is very important.

Looking at the CCSS speaking and listening strand, we can see that learning feedback skills from us will be critical for student success. The speaking and listening strand will have a significant impact on student learning, especially for struggling students. The comprehension and collaboration standards emphasize that students need to be self-directed learners. They need to not only read and write, but also articulate what they are learning to others. For example, the first part of standard one in the grade 6 speaking and listening strand requires students to "engage effectively in a range of collaborative discussions (one-on-one, in groups, and teacher-led) with diverse partners on grade 6 topics, texts, and issues, building on others' ideas and expressing their own clearly" (CCSSI, 2010). When learners are focused on their thinking, they will be better prepared to express their own ideas. The same standard goes on to include four more points, including one that requires students to "follow rules for collegial discussions, set specific goals and deadlines, and define individual roles as needed." This clearly calls for student-directed, independent learning. It is the students who need to do this work, not the teachers.

Going back to standard one in the grade 6 speaking and listening strand, one section of that standard requires that students "pose and respond to specific questions with elaboration and detail by making comments that contribute to the topic, text, or issue under discussion." As teachers, we need to ask better questions—more higher-order thinking questions—and we need to allow time for students to think and respond. Further, we must remember that our students also need to pose their own questions. Learning the skill of writing or asking a good question takes practice. Students need to become able to articulate, in speech as well as in writing, good questions that move from lower-order thinking to higher-order thinking. Identifying together how the learning has happened enables future learning and helps to ensure student success.

Metacognitive work is accomplished informally in conversation. These conversations are richer if the student has done some thinking prior to the meeting. Once again it is important to note that these skills may be very new to some students. Exhibits 2.5, 2.6, and 2.7 provide excellent checklists that can guide both student and teacher reflection. These checklists, created by Jody Hansen—teacher, instructional coach, and champion for learning—continue to help teachers and learners focus their thinking.

Exhibit 2.5 demonstrates that conversations about becoming an independent learner are not confined to older learners; there is a primary model as well. What is important is that these checklists become conversations between the teacher and student. The impact of this feedback is realized as we ask our students follow-up questions. For learners, the real power of those questions is in the teacher really listening to the answers. As students and teachers return to Hattie's three questions (2012)—Where am I going? How am I going there? and What next?—if students have become effective at self-monitoring, they have clarity about how to take their learning forward. This may not happen in our first conversations about their learning, but it will happen.

Skills of Independence Checklist—Early Grades

Skills of Independence
Student Edition

_____ I can get materials.

_____ I can work quietly.

_____ I can follow the rules.

_____ I can move safely around the room.

_____ I can work by myself.

_____ I can work with a friend.

_____ I can follow directions.

_____ I can make good choices with school property.

_____ I can help clean up when it is time.

_____ I can show my teacher I am listening.

_____ I can take care of myself.

_____ I can play safely.

_____ I can tell others about my learning.

Skills of Independence Checklist—Middle and Upper Grades

Skills of Independence
Student Edition

_____ I can get the materials I need for an activity.

_____ I can locate and work in an appropriate space.

_____ I can follow classroom rules and directions for tasks.

_____ I can move about the room without disturbing others.

_____ I can work without distracting others.

_____ I can return to my work space without interrupting others.

_____ I can complete a task according to directions.

_____ I can record my assignment scores on a chart to show my learning.

_____ I can use materials in a way that is respectful so that I can use them later.

_____ I can make the best use of my materials, using them without waste.

_____ I can return materials to the appropriate place.

_____ I can move from one activity to the next appropriately.

_____ I can make appropriate activity choices when choices are available.

_____ I can go to the appropriate resource at the appropriate time.

_____ I can respond appropriately to our classroom attention-getting signal.

_____ I can take care of my personal needs according to our classroom procedures.

_____ I can budget my time appropriately on a task.

_____ I can evaluate my work according to a rubric or set criteria.

BOOK FIVE
EXHIBIT
2.7

Skills of Independence Checklist—Teacher Edition

Skills of Independence
Teacher Edition

The following are examples of skills that students may need in the classroom to create a good working atmosphere. You may add others that students should learn.

_____ Getting materials needed.

_____ Going to an appropriate work space.

_____ Following rules and directions for tasks.

_____ Moving about the room without disturbing others.

_____ Working without distracting others.

_____ Returning to work space after interruption.

_____ Completing task according to criteria.

_____ Recording data needed upon completing task.

_____ Using materials in a manner allowing later use.

_____ Conserving materials.

_____ Returning materials appropriately.

_____ Moving to next activity appropriately.

_____ Making appropriate activity choices when choices are available.

_____ Going to appropriate resource at appropriate time.

_____ Responding appropriately to teacher's attention-getting signal.

_____ Taking care of personal needs according to class procedures.

_____ Budgeting time appropriately.

_____ Self-evaluating work according to set criteria.

If we are going to help students succeed at this challenging work, we will again need to be very aware of our own thinking and learning patterns.

WE CAN ONLY GIVE AWAY
WHAT WE ALREADY HAVE

It is often hard for us to recall what we were like at the beginning of our own learning process. Here are a few examples from my own conversations. Recently I talked with a teacher whom I had also had as a student back in her high school years. I listened to her talk about her current work and her frustration that she wasn't changing fast enough. I was able to remind her of the struggles she had overcome as the young student I had seen years before. Another teacher I worked with had started his fifth year of teaching, and we could talk about the changes since his first year. Another former student was in need of help solving a problem. As we talked, I asked what similarities there were between this challenge and one from earlier in her high school career. She was able to tell me of the steps taken in the past challenge, and as we reviewed the changes in her mindset, the increased ease with which she approached the problem and then applied that to her new challenge became apparent.

Who comes to your mind? Perhaps it's a person who gave you some important feedback. Or it's a person to whom you were able to give just the right feedback at the right time. Our self-awareness is central to giving authentic, helpful feedback. Here are a few questions to ponder before giving feedback:

- Where am I in my own mindset right now?
- Have I decided to keep growing, and am I taking actions that lead to continued growth?
- Is my feedback authentically designed to engage the learner in moving forward?
- What do I learn about myself as I reflect on the perspective of this chapter?
- What will I incorporate into my practice?

We can only give away what we have, and so we will continue to give feedback the same way we always have unless we make conscious choices to change. Let's be more intentional in our giving of feedback.

SUMMARY

Students need the hope that quality feedback provides. Teachers inviting, giving, and using effective feedback with their students transforms student achievement, and effective feedback has a critical role in moving struggling students forward to success with the CCSS. Through feedback, students are made aware of both what they have learned and what the next steps are to continue learning.

The Common Core calls for focused, sustained work to master central content and skills. When students become convinced that their efforts to learn will lead to success, they will become more motivated and focused. Real growth comes when students are empowered to take responsibility for their own learning.

The quality and timing of teacher feedback plays an important role in students' success. For educators, seeing students grow and realizing that they had a part to play brings both meaning and joy. Recalling these times helps provide the motivation to keep going. Let's give our students the effective feedback they need to learn and move forward.

References

Barth, R. (1990). *Improving schools from within.* San Francisco, CA: Jossey-Bass.

Common Core State Standards Initiative (CCSSI). (2010). *Common core state standards.* Retrieved from www.corestandards.org

Costa, A. L., & Kallick, B. (Eds.). (2012). *Habits of mind across the curriculum.* Alexandria, VA: ASCD.

Dean, C., Hubbell, E., Pitler, H., & Stone, B. (2012). *Classroom instruction that works* (2nd ed.). Alexandria, VA: ASCD.

Dweck, C. (2006). *Mindset.* New York, NY: Ballantine Books.

Feedback. (n.d.). In *Merriam-Webster's online dictionary.* Retrieved from www.merriam-webster.com/dictionary/feedback

Hattie, J. (2009). *Visible learning.* New York, NY: Routledge.

Hattie, J. (2012). *Visible learning for teachers.* New York, NY: Routledge.

Nuthall, G. (2007). *The hidden lives of learners.* Wellington, New Zealand: Nzcer Press.

Palmer, P. (2007). *Courage to teach.* San Francisco, CA: Jossey-Bass.

Reeves, D. B. (2011). *Navigating implementation of the common core state standards.* Englewood, CO: Lead + Learn Press.

Ritchhart, R., Church, M., & Morrison, K. (2011). *Making thinking visible.* San Francisco, CA: Jossey-Bass.

Willingham, D. (2009). *Why don't students like school?* San Francisco, CA: Jossey-Bass.

Willis, J. (2008). *How your child learns best.* Naperville, IL: Sourcebooks.

CHAPTER THREE

Scaffolding Instruction for the Common Core State Standards

Linda A. Gregg

Scaffolding can take many forms. When we speak of buildings, scaffolding refers to the structures that are built next to the building to provide layers of support during construction. The construction manager interprets a blueprint to decide what needs to be done. The scaffolding provides a level of support for the workers and for the materials so that the project can be successfully completed without the workers toppling. When construction is complete, the scaffolding is removed; its support is no longer needed.

Instructional scaffolding works the same way. The teacher has a firm understanding of what all of the students need to know and be able to do, which is typically taken from the Common Core State Standards (the blueprint). The primary focus is on the essential skills and concepts that all students need to know and be able to do. Teachers skillfully increase the level of support (the scaffolding) needed by each student during the learning process and adroitly fade the scaffolding as the students gain skills and understanding.

This chapter contains concrete, step-by-step examples of the process of scaffolding instruction aligned with the Common Core standards, including "unwrapping" a sample Common Core State Standard, following the steps for scaffolding as they relate to the specific standard, and providing specific scaffolding suggestions and practical tips and reminders to make scaffolding a natural part of high-quality instruction.

SCAFFOLDING AND THE COMMON CORE

The purpose of scaffolding is to provide support to students who require an additional layer of assistance in order to receive the most benefit from the initial instruction.

The Common Core State Standards provide guidance on what concepts students need to know and which skills they need, but they do not provide direct guidance on how teachers should teach. For the majority of students, the initial modeling, demonstration, high-leverage questioning, and constant feedback will yield proficiency. There are some students, however, who struggle or need differentiated support with new concepts and skills. For students learning English for the first time, many of the terms, expressions, procedures, and concepts in school may be new and may present a struggle. Students eligible for special education services may require scaffolding in one or more areas of instruction based on their Individualized Education Programs. Gifted students also benefit from scaffolding, which can help move them to higher levels of learning commensurate with their talents or intellectual abilities. There are also students who are "unclassified" struggling learners. Typically, these struggling learners do not qualify for any of the aforementioned categories, but the teacher may notice that these students need additional academic support in one or more areas of learning.

SCAFFOLDING SEQUENCE

The scaffolding process begins with selecting the standard required of the students and providing initial high-quality instruction. Once the teacher has established where students are in their learning from pre-assessment and observation, differentiation and scaffolding strategies should be used to support struggling learners, and then gradually faded out when students have mastered the skills and concepts. Students should be made aware of the strategies being used to support them as well. Making the strategy clearly visible to the students empowers them to understand the connection between the standard and their new scaffolding tools to help them generalize skills across the curriculum and achieve the required concepts and skills listed within an individual standard or multiple standards.

The following scaffolding steps provide a roadmap through the process, but scaffolding work doesn't end at the last step: it is recommended that ongoing collaborative practice, discussion, and feedback be used to constantly hone the skill and keep scaffolding in the forefront of the teacher's toolkit.

Step 1. Select the prioritized learning target from the Common Core State Standards.

Step 2. Determine what the students need to know and be able to do from the selected standard ("unwrapping").

Step 3. Examine the level of rigor.

Step 4. Provide high-quality explicit direct instruction.

Step 5. Assess student proficiency at strategic intervals before, during, and after initial instruction.

Step 6. Determine the level of scaffolding needed by targeted students.

Step 7. Determine the time and method of fading out the scaffolding supports.

Step 8. Establish monitoring probes to ensure that students are independent.

Remember, the Common Core State Standards specify the concepts that all students must know and the skills they must have, but it is the instructor's decision how to make sure proper scaffolding and differentiation are provided for students.

EXAMPLE ONE:
ELEMENTARY MATHEMATICS—DIVISION

Step 1: Select the Learning Target

The relevant Common Core standard is the starting point for scaffolding. It specifies what students need to know and be able to do. Scaffolding does not alter the standard itself to accommodate students' varied learning methods or speeds; it provides support so that all students can reach proficiency with the same standard.

Step 2: Determine What the Students Need to Know and Be Able to Do

Clearly defining the skills and knowledge expected of students is crucial. This ensures that the instruction is focused and meets the level of rigor required by the standard. Larry Ainsworth, in *"Unwrapping" the Standards* (2003), describes in detail the process by which standards can be "unwrapped" so that the specific skills and concepts within them are drawn into focus. Exhibit 3.1 gives an example of an "unwrapped" standard.

After the standard is "unwrapped" and the skills and concepts are listed, advanced users of this process may define the Essential Questions and Big Ideas for the standard as well during this step.

BOOK FIVE
EXHIBIT
3.1

Sample Standard for Elementary Mathematics

Standard 4.NBT.6: Find whole-number quotients and remainders with up to four-digit dividends and one-digit divisors using strategies based on place value, the properties of operations, and/or the relationship between multiplication and division. Illustrate and explain the calculation by using equations, rectangular arrays, and/or area models.

Concepts: (what students need to know)—nouns shown in the standard	Skills: (what students need to be able to do)—verbs shown in the standard
• Whole-number quotients and remainders • Place value • Properties of operations • Relationship between multiplication and division • Calculation • Equations, rectangular arrays, and/or area models	**Find** (Bloom level 2) (DOK level 1) **Use** (Bloom level 3) (DOK level 1) **Illustrate** (Bloom level 3) (DOK level 1) **Explain** (Bloom level 5) (DOK level 1)

Tip: Consider weaving the skills specified in the standards throughout the lesson. The activities provided by the teacher should give students ample opportunity to use the concepts and perform the skills, and high-leverage questions and specific feedback should be offered to students to help them use the concepts and perform the skills throughout the instructional period. Students should be able to make connections and ultimately demonstrate their ability to independently use the concepts and perform the skills in a variety of contexts.

Step 3: Examine the Level of Rigor

Determining the level of rigor required by the standard can be accomplished using Bloom's taxonomy and/or Webb's Depth of Knowledge (DOK) levels (Exhibits 3.2 and 3.3). Determining the cognitive level will help both the teacher and the student understand the level of expectation for the standard. Cognitive levels also help the teacher determine the level of activities, questions, and feedback to provide to the students and the type of scaffolding that will be needed for students to achieve proficiency.

BOOK FIVE EXHIBIT 3.2 **Bloom's Revised Taxonomy**

Skill Level (what students should be able to do)	
Rigor	**Skill(s)**
6	Creating
5	Evaluating
4	Analyzing
3	Applying
2	Understanding
1	Remembering

Source: Adapted from Anderson and Krathwohl, 2000.

BOOK FIVE EXHIBIT 3.3 — Norman Webb's Depth of Knowledge (DOK) Levels

Depth of Knowledge (DOK)		
Skill Level (what students should be able to do)		**Examples of verbs associated with CCSS**
Rigor	**Skill(s)**	
4	Extended Thinking	Prove, create, analyze, critique, apply concepts, synthesize, connect, design
3	Strategic Thinking	Revise, assess, hypothesize, cite evidence, draw conclusions, revise, differentiate
2	Skills/Concepts	Classify, organize, predict, interpret, infer, show, summarize, cause/effect
1	Recall	Recognize, match name, report, illustrate, arrange, tell, memorize, identify, list

Source: Adapted from Webb, 2005.

For some students, the instructor may feel that the level of rigor described in the standard could be increased to the next level. Exhibit 3.1 includes the Bloom's taxonomy and Webb's DOK levels of the skills in the example standard. Exhibit 3.2 lists the cognitive levels in the revised Bloom's taxonomy, and Exhibit 3.3 lists DOK levels developed by Norman Webb.

Step 4: Provide High-Quality Explicit Direct Instruction

Before beginning to scaffold the instruction, it is important that the teacher deliver initial high-quality instruction to all of the students. Explicit direct instruction is key to student understanding. Teachers should demonstrate, model, use visuals, ask high-leverage questions, and give students multiple opportunities for practice and appropriate feedback. Feedback given to students during instruction should be targeted to the level-specific tasks. Carol Dweck reminds us, in her remarkable book *Mindset* (2006), that students require specific and constructive feedback, and Robert Marzano (2007) advocates using targeted feedback aimed at providing the student with guidance for next steps.

Explicit instruction strategies include, but are not limited to, the strategies shown in Exhibit 3.4. It is important to distinguish between a strategy and an activity: A strategy represents the teacher's actions. An activity delineates what the student will do. High-quality instruction focuses on adult actions—on what the instructor does to promote learning.

When beginning this process, the teacher should begin with one instructional strategy, such as the use of visual demonstration or modeling, and gradually add strategies as needed. An example of one of the strategies is provided in Exhibit 3.5.

BOOK
FIVE
EXHIBIT
3.4

Strategies for Explicit Direct Instruction

Strategy	Description
Entrance Slip	The instructor may use an **entrance slip** as a way of determining what students already know about the subject (continuing with the example in Exhibit 3.1, the topic is "division") and their primary level of proficiency. The entrance slip may be one to three problems that students complete before the lesson begins, or it may ask students to explain the mathematical concept in words. It can also be provided at the end of the previous day to allow the teacher more time to analyze the baseline of student proficiency. It can be used as a "do now" or "bell ringer" at the beginning of class.
K-W-H-L Chart	The instructor may use a **K-W-H-L Chart** to see what the students already know **(K)** about division, and what they want to know **(W)**. The instructor will provide **(H)**—how students will learn the concepts and skills (what resources they will use) to enhance the learning. **(L)** stands for specifically what students have learned. The chart should remain visible to the class during the entire unit, and beyond, if applicable. Students may also have their own copies of the chart to promote metacognition.
Visuals	The instructor may use **visuals** by initially writing the algorithm on the chalkboard or white board or projecting it. The teacher will write out the procedural steps so the students will be able to see the process clearly. Visual learners will benefit from seeing the work as the teacher demonstrates it.
Think-Aloud	The instructor may use a **think-aloud** strategy, in which the teacher verbally describes her thinking to the students as she is working on the math example. Auditory learners will benefit from hearing how the teacher is thinking as she works through the example for the class.

Continued

Strategies for Explicit Direct Instruction *(Continued)*

Strategy	Description
Whole Brain Teaching	The instructor may use a **"whole-brain teaching" strategy,** in which students have the opportunity to provide choral, turn-and-teach-a-peer, and total physical responses (TPR) to the teacher's instruction.
Acronyms (Example in Exhibit 3.5)	The instructor may provide an **acronym** to the students for division as a method of helping them to remember the multiple steps of the process.
Think-Write-Pair -Share	The instructor may offer multiple opportunities for students to use the metacognitive process, such as **think-pair-share** or **think-write-pair-share.**
Standards-Based Vocabulary	The instructor should use **standards-based vocabulary.** The teacher will constantly model standards-based vocabulary; in this case, words such as **"quotients,"** "remainders," "digit," "dividends," and "divisors" are used throughout the lesson and allow students a chance to share their thinking and practice saying and applying the new vocabulary in as many ways as possible. Students may create a math strategies and/or vocabulary booklet, index cards, vocabulary web, nonlinguistic representation, or comparison matrix. Sometimes students miss problems on state assessments because they have not been exposed to a robust vocabulary. If teachers use words such as "take away" rather than "subtraction," "times" rather than "multiply," or "regrouping" rather than "borrowing," students may struggle to generalize or substitute the term and may not recognize the standards-based words when they are presented in a different context, such as a state assessment. Students will learn the vocabulary from the standards when it is explained, used frequently, and modeled.

Continued

BOOK FIVE EXHIBIT 3.4

Strategies for Explicit Direct Instruction *(Continued)*

Strategy	Description
Constructive Feedback	The instructor should be explicit in delivering the instruction and also in providing **constructive feedback** that allows the students to see what they are doing well and what they need to do better.
High-Leverage Questioning	During the lesson, the teacher may provide **high-leverage questioning** while skillfully checking for student understanding. This means the instructor should: 1. Ask questions that match the level of rigor from the standard. In our example, the teacher would look for opportunities to ask questions about "using" and "performing" various division operations. 2. Provide appropriate wait-time—a few extra seconds or a pre-arranged prompt for individual students—so that students have time to process the information. 3. Cue visual or auditory guidance. Another component of high-leverage questioning is students' ability to use metacognition to think about their thinking so they can internalize, or "own," the skill or concept and move toward independence.
Choral Practice	The instructor may provide ample opportunities for the students to actively participate in the lesson through **choral practice** (small or large group of students reads designated passages of the text in unison).
Modeling	The instructor may **model** the expectations for the students so they can see exactly what they should do before beginning. This provides the students with an exemplar.

Continued

BOOK FIVE EXHIBIT 3.4

Strategies for Explicit Direct Instruction *(Continued)*

Strategy	Description
Demon-stration	The instructor may **demonstrate** how the skill is to be performed.
Pre-teaching	The instructor may provide instruction to the students prior to the small- or whole-group lesson. Pre-teaching may include a brief demonstration, explanation of a handout, or vocabulary review.
Explicit Examples	The instructor may give students the opportunity to work with realia (real, tangible items) when possible, to connect the lesson to real life and to the students' background knowledge.
Advance Organizers	Examples include but are not limited to: pre-printed examples, strategy notebooks, charts, outlines, and mind maps.

Example of Acronym Memory Device

Does McDonald's Serve Cheese Burgers?

Have students write DMSCB on the left side of their papers before starting the division problem. Write a long division problem using only one digit in the divisor. Demonstrate for students that each letter has a step, and remind them that although "cheeseburger" is spelled as one word, they'll treat it as two words for the purposes of the long division memory device.

Does **M**cDonald's **S**erve **C**heese **B**urgers?

D is for division.

M is for multiplication.

S is for subtraction.

C is for checking your answer.

B is for "bringing it down."

The strategies selected by the instructor should be determined by student need, based on the pre-assessment. Anita Archer and Charles Hughes, authors of *Explicit Instruction* (2010), point out that we must provide instruction that matches the individual needs of the students. Students may, in fact, require different types of instruction at different times.

Step 5: Assess Student Proficiency at Strategic Intervals Before, During, and After Initial Instruction

While the instructor is providing high-quality instruction that includes explicit direct instruction and differentiation to address the needs of individuals and small groups of students, it is important to assess students' needs along the way. This is done before, during, and after initial instruction. Before instruction, teachers can use entrance slips, K-W-H-L charts, or informal high-leverage questioning to determine which students may require a form of scaffolding following the formal lesson. Assessment may also take place during the lesson. For example, students can demonstrate their knowledge on a white board, respond to prompts or learning probes, take written or oral quizzes, or answer high-leverage questions on electronic devices. After instruction, the instructor provides assessments designed to determine if students are now proficient or require additional assistance. For example, the teacher may provide projects, short-cycle assessments in the form of selected-response (multiple choice, true or false, fill in the blank), or constructed-response prompts. Students may also be assigned performance tasks to demonstrate their mastery or proficiency.

Step 6: Determine the Level of Scaffolding Needed by Targeted Students

It is necessary for educators to return to the standard frequently to make sure that they are providing support for the requirements of the standard. In this example (division), students are expected to use place value and properties of operations to perform multi-digit arithmetic.

In our example, the problem is 2579 divided by 5. Several students in class responded with 511 as their answer. Initially, the instructor was puzzled. The instructor shared the results of the pre-assessment (a three-question entrance slip) with a grade-level Data Team. The team was unable to determine how several students wrote the same responses. They provided two suggestions:

1. There were four students who had the same response; ask them to demonstrate and verbally explain how they got the answer.

2. Observe the students as they work through the operation.

To most efficiently scaffold instruction, one should carefully analyze student needs to know which skills and concepts require a layer (scaffold) of support. If we go back to the original example of scaffolding a structure, consider that the scaffolding is only needed around parts of the building that are not yet complete. The instructor may have determined that students need more support with a particular concept. In our example, the teacher may determine that the four students are struggling with place value.

Step 7: Determine the Time and Method of Fading Out the Scaffolding Supports

The instructor should determine the time and method for fading of scaffolding supports on a case-by-case basis. For example, when young children are learning to ride a bicycle, sometimes parents provide them with training wheels (a type of scaffolding) to help them as they learn to balance the bicycle. After the children appear to balance and perform well with the training wheels, the parents will remove the training wheels, but they continue to move briskly alongside the children temporarily until the children have proven themselves capable of maintaining a safe balance for independent cycling.

Step 8: Establish Monitoring Probes to Ensure that Students are Independent

Once the scaffolding has been faded out, it is important to continue to monitor students' performance to make sure they remain on track. To continue with the bicycle analogy, when the child begins riding well, the training wheels are removed, but the parents typically do not just turn their backs on the child! They establish monitoring probes to ensure that the child can ride independently. The probe in this case may be observation: How steady is the child on the bike? Does the child still need additional support? Is it a smooth ride, or still a bit wobbly? Rather than placing the training wheels back on the bicycle, the parent will typically end up running alongside the child for a few seconds, or providing verbal feedback, encouragement, and verbal guidance from the side.

EXAMPLE TWO: GRADES 9–10 ELA—INFORMATIONAL TEXT

Steps 1, 2, and 3

Exhibit 3.6 shows steps one through three of the scaffolding process:

Step 1. Select the learning target from the Common Core State Standards.

Step 2. Determine what the students need to know and be able to do.

Step 3. Examine the level of rigor.

Grades 9–10 Informational Text

RIT.9–10.7: Analyze various accounts of a subject told in different mediums (e.g., as a person's life story told in both print and multimedia), determining which details are emphasized in each account.

Concepts: (what students need to know)—Nouns shown in the standard	Skills: (what students need to be able to do)—Verbs shown in the standard
• Accounts of a subject	**Analyze** (Bloom level 4) (DOK level 4)
• Person's life story	
• Print and multimedia	**Determine** (Bloom level 5) (DOK level 3)
• Emphasized details in an account	

Tip: Consider using this English language arts standard across the curriculum in courses such as social studies, art, and music. Students should be able to make connections and ultimately demonstrate their independent ability to use and perform the concepts in a variety of contexts when possible.

Steps 4, 5, and 6

Step 4. Provide high-quality explicit direct instruction.

Step 5. Assess student proficiency at strategic intervals before, during, and after initial instruction.

Step 6. Determine the level of scaffolding needed for targeted students in order to help them benefit appropriately from the instruction.

In this example, the instructor will use a historical figure such as President Abraham Lincoln as the subject about which students must analyze various accounts told in different mediums and determine which details are emphasized in each account.

Remember from the previous example that explicit instruction should begin with examples or demonstration, modeling, visuals, high-leverage questioning, and allowing students an opportunity for practice using the new concepts and skills with appropriate feedback. Explicit instruction for this standard may include strategies such as the ones listed in Exhibit 3.7. When beginning this process, the teacher should start with one instructional strategy, such as the use of visuals or graphic organizers; additional strategies may be added as needed. Exhibit 3.8 is an example of a graphic organizer that may be used in the classroom.

To build scaffolding for this particular standard, the instructor may decide to teach one section of the standard at a time.

Students may not require the same level of scaffolding for every assignment. The instructor must make a predetermination of students' needs through observation, listening to student responses to high-quality questions, entrance slips, Individualized Education Program (IEP) modifications, or determining the stu-

BOOK FIVE
EXHIBIT
3.7

Examples of Strategies Used for Explicit Instruction and Scaffolding

Analyze various accounts of a subject told in different mediums such as a person's life story in both print and multimedia.

Strategy	Description
Pre-Teaching Vocabulary	The instructor may use a graphic organizer, pre-printed information, leveled reading material, acronym, or color-coded text.
Graphic Organizers (Example of comparison matrix is shown in Exhibit 3.8)	The instructor may use a word wheel, thesaurus, Venn diagram, or comparison matrix.
Electronic Medium	http://www.whitehouse.gov (Presidential Facts) http://www.ipl.org/div/potus/ (Drexel University's College of Information Science & Technology) http://www.teachingwithlincoln.com/ (Library of Congress, Teaching with Primary Sources) YouTube videos (teachers must prescreen) *Lincoln* movie trailers http://www.Teachertube.com (Video Archive) http://www.Annenberg.org (Video Archive) http://www.PBS.org (Videos Archive)
Think-Aloud	The instructor may orally describe thoughts about each aspect of the subject (Lincoln). Students may turn to their partner and repeat.
Visuals	Google Images, Yahoo, posters, textbooks, Cooliris (www.cooliris.com)

Determine which details are emphasized in each account.

Basic Facts	The teacher may replay President Lincoln's communication style, geography, timeline of historical events, character, and accomplishments.
Compare and Contrast	The teacher may select another president and compare/contrast with Lincoln the basic facts.

BOOK FIVE
EXHIBIT 3.8
Sample Comparison Matrix

	Commu-nication	Geography	Accomplish-ments	Character	
Abraham Lincoln					
Andrew Johnson					

dents' language status. Once the students' instructional needs are analyzed, the instructor can determine the level of scaffolding needed for targeted students in order to help them benefit appropriately from the instruction. A few students may initially require several of the instructional strategies with intensive scaffolding to help them.

SUMMARY

One size does not fit all! Struggling students frequently require explicit instruction that includes developing a clear understanding of the vocabulary, a gradual introduction of information, multiple opportunities to practice, and planned fading of the scaffolding supports that have been created for the learner. This type of instruction can take many forms, as discussed in this chapter. Scaffolding may also provide enhancement strategies for students that are ready to move to high levels of skill/concept attainment. In addition, the instructor must be aware of the need to assess and monitor the student's level of independence while establishing and then fading the scaffolds as appropriate.

The recommended sequence for scaffolding is:

Step 1. Select the learning target from the Common Core State Standards.

Step 2. Determine what the students need to know and be able to do ("unwrap" the standard).

Step 3. Examine the level of rigor.

Step 4. Provide high-quality, explicit instruction.

Step 5. Assess student proficiency at strategic intervals before, during, and after initial instruction.

Step 6. Determine the level of scaffolding needed by targeted students.

Step 7. Determine the time and method of fading out the scaffolding supports.

Step 8. Establish monitoring probes to ensure that students are independent.

A variety of instructional strategies can be used to scaffold learning for struggling students; the important thing is that the strategies be chosen specifically to meet the needs of the particular students who require learning support or enhanced instruction.

Mild, moderate, or intensive scaffolding may be used to help struggling learners navigate the Common Core State Standards with confidence. Remember to discuss the strategies being used with the students so they understand, for example, that the "training wheels" being provided may be used as an initial scaffolding strategy, but that they will be removed as soon as possible. Students will also need to understand that the teacher will continue to monitor and support their efforts as much as possible until the ride is smoother and completed successfully. Some students may not need the intensity of "training wheels" at the beginning, but may require constructive guidance through feedback, prompts, or verbal assistance. In any instance of planned mild, moderate, or intensive support, all students should be provided with what they need to obtain success with the Common Core State Standards.

References

Ainsworth, L. (2003). *"Unwrapping" the standards: A simple process to make standards manageable.* Englewood, CO: Lead + Learn Press.

Anderson, L. W., & Krathwohl, D. R. (Eds.). (2000). *A taxonomy for learning, teaching, and assessing: A revision of Bloom's taxonomy of educational objectives.* Upper Saddle River, NJ: Pearson.

Archer, A., & Hughes, C. A. (2010). *Explicit instruction: Effective and efficient teaching.* New York, NY: Guilford.

Bloom, B. (1956). *Taxonomy of educational objectives.* New York, NY: Longman.

Dweck, C. S. (2006). *Mindset: The new psychology of success.* New York, NY: Random House.

Marzano, R. (2007). *The art and science of teaching: A comprehensive framework for effective instruction.* Alexandria, VA: ASCD.

Webb, N. L. (2005). Depth of knowledge (DOK) levels. Retrieved from http://dese.mo.gov/divimprove/sia/msip/DOK_Chart.pdf

CHAPTER FOUR

Building Vocabulary Knowledge So All Students Can Tell Stories

Mary F. Piper

Stories are the way people communicate their thoughts and ideas, and people use words to tell these stories. The vocabulary used to tell stories has worth, increases achievement, and signifies power. First, words have value. An extensive vocabulary has greater value than most material possessions. Another person can take away your belongings but cannot take away your words. It is important for people not only to protect their "good word," but also to use words correctly. Second, vocabulary attainment is an indicator of achievement in school and in life. Robust instruction improves not only students' vocabulary, but also their reading comprehension skills (Stahl and Fairbanks, 1986; Beck, McKeown, and Kucan, 2002). Additionally, a large and rich vocabulary is a trait of an educated person (Beck, McKeown, and Kucan, 2002). Finally, vocabulary is a source of power. Purves (1990) found that societies separate and segregate through the use of academic tone, register, and vocabulary. With the advent of the Common Core State Standards, it is time to provide research-based vocabulary instruction so that all students, especially those who struggle in school, can develop both oral and written vocabularies that allow them to tell their stories.

RESEARCH

Research on effective vocabulary instruction is plentiful and is getting renewed attention as educators grapple with the Common Core State Standards. Stahl and Fairbanks' 1986 meta-analysis found that vocabulary instruction has a mean effect size of 0.97. Additionally, the effect size of vocabulary instruction's impact on reading comprehension of passages in standardized tests was 0.30. Educators know that students' word knowledge is critical to academic achievement and reading comprehension. Research that substantiates this knowledge provides support for effective vocabulary instruction in classrooms at all grade levels across all content areas.

Even though the effects of vocabulary instruction are well known, the time dedicated to teaching vocabulary was found to be approximately just 6 percent of school time, with only 1.4 percent of time in classes other than language arts committed to vocabulary development (Scott, Jamieson-Noel, and Asselin, 2003). It is surprising to observe so little time dedicated to quality vocabulary instruction. The 6 percent of dedicated time in English language arts and 1.4 percent of time in other content areas will not allow students to master the knowledge and skills demanded by the rigorous Common Core State Standards.

Effective vocabulary instruction emphasizes definitional and contextual (or mixed-methods) strategies, includes multiple exposures in different contexts, and uses keyword mnemonics due to the significant effects of this particular strategy.

Watts (1995) observed elementary classrooms and reached the following four conclusions about vocabulary instruction:

1. Teachers controlled conversations about word meanings.

2. Teachers used limited strategies to teach vocabulary.

3. Research-based, effective vocabulary instruction was not established.

4. Teachers believed vocabulary instruction was important to their classes or courses but did not see the benefit of this instruction in terms of students' learning trajectory in a specific discipline or multiple disciplines.

Marzano (2004) identifies eight characteristics of effective vocabulary instruction:

1. Vocabulary instruction does not rely on definitions.

2. Linguistic and nonlinguistic representations of words lead to improved word learning.

3. Vocabulary is developed through multiple exposures.

4. Teaching word parts (affixes and roots) improves student understanding of vocabulary terms.

5. Differentiated instruction is required for students to learn different kinds of words.

6. Discourse aids in word learning.

7. Games and word play help students learn words.

8. Direct instruction should focus on words that students need to know to be academically successful.

Shanahan and Shanahan (2008) propose a model of literacy development based on "tiers," much like the Beck, McKeown, and Kucan (2002) tiered vocabulary framework. The Shanahan framework assumes that reading and writing instruction must become more focused on disciplinary literacy (described in Exhibit 4.1) if students are to learn from the texts in various domains.

Lee and Spratley (2010) added to Shanahan and Shanahan's (2008) framework by reporting that adolescents struggle with text due to: a) vocabulary; b) topic and text structure knowledge; c) knowing what to do when comprehension breaks down; and

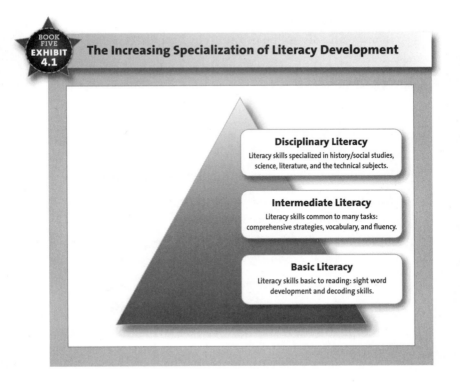

BOOK FIVE EXHIBIT 4.1   **The Increasing Specialization of Literacy Development**

Disciplinary Literacy
Literacy skills specialized in history/social studies, science, literature, and the technical subjects.

Intermediate Literacy
Literacy skills common to many tasks: comprehensive strategies, vocabulary, and fluency.

Basic Literacy
Literacy skills basic to reading: sight word development and decoding skills.

d) proficiency in monitoring their own reading comprehension. Nagy and Townsend (2012) continue to focus on vocabulary as important to disciplinary literacy when they postulate that words are tools, and proficiency with academic language provides access to knowledge, improves thinking skills in specific disciplines, and improves general achievement. As research continues in the field of disciplinary literacy, advances about effective vocabulary instruction should develop and impact instruction.

VOCABULARY AND THE COMMON CORE

The Common Core anchor standards for vocabulary appear in the language strand and are as follows (Common Core State Standards Initiative, 2010c):

- Use word attack strategies to determine the meanings of unknown or unfamiliar words in all situations (L.CCR.4).
- Apply their understanding of the various meanings of words (denotations, connotations, nuances) and figurative language (L.CCR.5).
- Acquire and use increasingly complex academic vocabulary in reading, writing, speaking, and listening (L.CCR.6).

Vocabulary does not receive much attention in the Common Core State Standards documents. First, the vocabulary standards in the Common Core are not as specific as other English language arts standards. Further, the information provided in Appendix A of the English language arts CCSS provides only cursory guidance.

Recommendations for applying the CCSS for English language learners (Common Core State Standards Initiative, 2010a) are barely defined in a three-page document. Suggestions for English language learners are additional time, more support, and aligned assessments. The Common Core's "Application to Students with Disabilities" document (Common Core State Standards Initiative, 2010b) is a two-page document that recommends additional supports and services, such as the following:

- Instructional supports based on Universal Design for Learning (UDL) principles.

- Individualized Education Programs (IEPs) that specify accommodations that do not change the standards but may change materials or procedures.

- Assistive technology devices and services to provide access to the general education curriculum.

Silver, Dewing, and Perini (2012) recommend focusing on vocabulary as an essential strategy for achieving success with the Common Core State Standards for the following reasons:

- Vocabulary is a foundation for improved literacy.

- Academic vocabulary is at the core of the Core.

- Vocabulary fuels learning.

Vocabulary instruction in classrooms has not been informed by research; during observations, researchers have found little change in classroom practice (Watts, 1995). It stands to reason that when all students do receive best practices vocabulary instruction, instruction will simultaneously improve for both the mainstream students and those who struggle. As Peery (2011) states, all three vocabulary standards have application across the disciplines, but due to limited direction, administrators and teachers need to not only study the standards but also find resources to meet the goals of the standards. It is wise to study the Common Core State Standards language standards, next generation assessments, and vocabulary research to identify instructional strategies that will lead to improved vocabulary development. An additional way to study the vocabulary standards is through building-level and instructional Data Teams. Blachowicz, Fisher, Ogle, and Watts-Taffe (2006) state that schools with effective vocabulary initiatives develop a common approach to word learning. Action research embedded in the Data Teams cycle will increase the chances that such a vocabulary initiative, as part of a school-wide literacy plan, will be formed to meet the needs of the community of students at all times and in all classrooms.

WHAT WORDS TO TEACH?

According to Vadasy & Nelson (2012), determining what words to teach can be accomplished in one of three ways. First, words can be determined by the frequency with which they occur in the English language. Second, vocabulary words can be taught in the sequence in which words are acquired. Last, vocabulary word lists can be established based on a tier approach. The Common Core State Standards outline the framework of Beck, McKeown, and Kucan (2002) as a way to identify vocabulary words for direct instruction. The "tiers," along with a basic description, are shown in Exhibit 4.2.

Beck, McKeown, and Kucan (2002) outline criteria for identifying tier two words:

• Importance and utility—Are the words useful? Will students see the words frequently in multiple disciplines?

BOOK FIVE EXHIBIT 4.2 **Vocabulary Tiers**

Tier	Description
Tier One	Everyday or basic words
Tier Two	General academic words; more likely to appear in written texts than in speech; used across a variety of disciplines; appear in informational texts, technical texts, and literary texts
Tier Three	Domain-specific words; frequency of use is low

Source: Adapted from Beck, McKeown, and Kucan, 2002.

- Instructional potential—Can students work with these words in numerous ways to develop deep knowledge of the terms? Can connections between the studied words and other related words and/or concepts be made?

- Conceptual understanding—Are the words needed to precisely communicate about a concept?

Marzano (2004) recommends creating customized, domain-specific academic word lists since these words are needed for academic success in each subject or class. Paynter, Bodrova, and Doty (2005) suggest selecting direct instruction words that have these characteristics: 1) words that have multiple meanings or words that could confuse students; 2) words that are new to students; and 3) words that are difficult to understand. Beck,

McKeown, and Kucan (2002) recommend direct instruction of tier two, or general academic, words. Tier two words should be a priority, since the recommendations of the Common Core State Standards are based on Beck, McKeown, and Kucan's (2002) work.

Initially, word lists must be developed, and some resources for creating customized word lists can be found in the Common Core State Standards, the CCSS text exemplars, basic word lists, domain-specific word lists, and next generation assessments. The Leadership and Learning Center advocates collaboration through Data Teams. Data Teams, organized by grade levels or departments, can draft word lists. These lists can then be reviewed by the building Data Team. The building Data Team review would naturally lead to prioritized word lists, since omissions, repetitions, and gaps among grade levels would be identified. Collaboration is critical in creating content-specific word lists, but most critical when creating tier two word lists for use throughout the school in all disciplines. Data Teams are based on the collaborative creation of Common Formative Assessments aligned to the Common Core State Standards. These Common Formative Assessments would assess both vocabulary and content knowledge.

RESEARCH-BASED
VOCABULARY INSTRUCTION

Stahl and Fairbanks (1986) found individualized vocabulary instruction to be the same as completing worksheets. Most students, including those who are young, can be skilled at completing worksheets with little thought given to the content or the concepts that are the objectives of the lesson. Scott, Jamieson-Noel, and Asselin (2003) further state:

The general use of rote learning and worksheet exercises: Rote learning and worksheets constrain vocabulary learning to the extent they are decontextualized and devoid of relevant connections to life or other curricular content. Such tasks ignore the importance of cognitive connections and the development of schematic knowledge. (p. 281)

Rote learning and worksheets are far from what is recommended by best practices vocabulary research. Beck, McKeown, and Kucan (2002) claim that robust vocabulary instruction is composed of these four critical elements:

1. Selecting tier two words to teach

2. Developing student-friendly definitions for these words

3. Engaging children in appealing, demanding, engaging activities in which they learn to access the meanings of words in multiple contexts

4. Finding more time during the day to devote to vocabulary instruction

Marzano (2004) acknowledges the importance of direct instruction but also recommends indirect vocabulary instruction to enhance background knowledge. The first prong of an indirect approach involves establishing a sustained silent reading program; students benefit from reading to build background knowledge. The second prong of the indirect approach is to increase language interaction, talking, and listening, which also generates knowledge creation.

Hattie (2009) found explicit instruction in vocabulary to have an effect size of 0.67 on achievement. This is considered a highly effective practice on his scale for improving student comprehension. Direct instruction's impact on student learning is estimated at an effect size of 0.59. Combining vocabulary instruction with direct instruction methodology should yield extraordinary gains in student achievement. Paynter, Bodrova, and Doty (2005) outlined a process that combines research-based instructional strategies and that is designed to provide six exposures to target words through direct instruction (p. 36):

1. The teacher identifies the new word and brings out the students' background knowledge.

2. The teacher explains the meaning of the new word in student-friendly terms.

3. Students generate their own explanations; teachers clarify any misconceptions.

4. Students create a visual representation of the new word.

5. Students engage in experiences that deepen their understanding of the new word.

6. Students engage in vocabulary games to help them remember the word and its meaning.

The research about effective vocabulary is robust and full of common-sense recommendations. Educators should collaborate and enact strategies that best fit their students' needs.

RECOMMENDATIONS FOR STRUGGLING LEARNERS

Lee and Spratley (2010) recommend generic and discipline-specific strategies for struggling readers (shown in Exhibit 4.3).

BOOK FIVE EXHIBIT 4.3   **Reading Strategies**

Generic "Good Reading" Strategies	Discipline-Specific Reading Strategies
• Set goals • Preread • Think about what you already know • Ask questions • Make predictions • Test predictions against the text • Reread • Monitor comprehension • Summarize	• Build prior knowledge • Build domain-specific vocabulary • Learn to break down complex sentences • Use knowledge of text structures and genres to predict main ideas and details • Map graphics against explanations in the text • Pose discipline-specific questions while reading • Compare claims and propositions across texts • Use norms for reasoning to evaluate claims

Source: Lee and Spratley, 2010.

These activities should lead to improved vocabulary as well as reading comprehension.

Generic vocabulary instruction, like generic reading strategy instruction, can be used before, during, and after literacy lessons. Generic vocabulary strategies, such as those recommended by Allen (2007), ensure that students learn strategies that can improve comprehension and content knowledge.

Discipline-specific vocabulary instruction would likewise mirror discipline-specific reading strategy instruction. Classroom teaching that embeds effective word learning in all lessons begins with building prior knowledge. Specific vocabulary strategy instruction would vary according to the demands of the discipline. This could be accomplished through cues and questions or the use of graphic organizers. Using knowledge of text structures and genres along with graphics during close reading could help students predict the most important ideas while reading or listening. Teachers who pose thought-provoking questions assist students in making inferences and spark the thinking of students as they engage with text or participate in discussions. This thinking could lead to the development of an argumentative stance while reading and writing, which is a critical element of the Common Core State Standards. Supports for those who struggle will ensure that all students benefit from generic and discipline-specific vocabulary instruction.

Vadasy and Nelson (2012) assume effective general education approaches are beneficial to students who struggle. In particular, these researchers emphasize robust vocabulary instruction (Beck, McKeown, and Kucan, 2002) and the Word Generation Program (www.wordgeneration.org).

Morphology instruction and keyword mnemonics are linked to large learning gains for all learners, but especially those who struggle (Hattie, 2009; Vadasy and Nelson, 2012). Morphology instruction involves understanding prefixes, suffixes, and roots, which helps students comprehend what is read. Morphology instruction during vocabulary lessons involves analyzing words for morphemes (prefixes, suffixes, and roots), thinking of meanings based upon word parts, and checking meaning within the text or conversation. Morphology instruction is critical for all students; those who struggle will need scaffolds and repeated practice. The result is improvements in decoding, spelling, inference skills, and word knowledge.

A keyword mnemonic is an aid to help students learn new words. Students make a connection between a new word and an image of a related word that is a "key" to remembering the new word. An example could be an image of geese for Greece since geese fly over the island of Greece. It is important to note that learning how to create a keyword mnemonic requires direct instruction. It is also important to point out that keyword mnemonics are best followed with other vocabulary strategies to provide multiple exposures to new words. Strategies like morphology instruction and keyword mnemonics are beneficial in assisting those who struggle with vocabulary acquisition in developing a larger vocabulary.

English language learners benefit from explicit vocabulary instruction that focuses on general academic words, provides multiple exposures, and develops the use of cognates (Paynter, Bodrova, and Doty, 2005; Blachowicz, Fisher, Ogle, and Watts-Taffe, 2006; Snow, Lawrence, and White, 2009; Kelley, Lesaux, Kieffer, and Faller, 2010). Cognates, which are words in two languages that share a similar meaning, spelling, and pronunciation, can benefit ELL students. Not all languages align with English, but English shares about 30 to 40 percent of cognates with Spanish. For ELLs, the link formed between the first and second language improves understanding or comprehension. Students can be introduced to more complex or multiple-meaning cognates as they progress through grade levels. Opportunities to use the words orally and in writing were provided in several successful vocabulary programs designed for English language learners (Snow, Lawrence, and White, 2009; Vadasy and Nelson, 2012).

SUMMARY

The Common Core State Standards are the result of the United States standards movement that has spanned the last 20 years. As the CCSS are put into practice throughout most of the United States, it is time to raise the level of rigor of vocabulary instruction.

As researchers and teachers continue on the lifelong journey of learning, disciplinary literacy has become the focus of learning across content areas and requires an emphasis on vocabulary instruction. As we know and have always known, vocabulary instruction aids student learning in all subjects. Vocabulary provides oral and written evidence of learning.

Proven models of vocabulary instruction can be implemented and adjusted to meet the context of a particular district and/or school. Improving vocabulary through research-based instruction is beneficial for those who do well in school, but especially for those who struggle. It is time to combine tools, the standards, and research-based vocabulary instruction so all students, especially those who struggle in school, can develop both oral and written vocabularies that allow them to tell their stories.

References

Allen, J. (2007). *Inside words: Tools for teaching academic vocabulary, grades 4–12*. Portland, ME: Stenhouse.

Beck, I. L., McKeown, M. G., & Kucan, L. (2002). *Bringing words to life: Robust vocabulary instruction*. New York, NY: Guilford.

Blachowicz, C. L. Z., Fisher, P. J. L., Ogle, D., & Watts-Taffe, S. (2006). Vocabulary: Questions from the classroom. *Reading Research Quarterly, 41*(4), 524–539.

Common Core State Standards Initiative (CCSSI). (2010a, June). *Common core state standards: Application of common core state sandards for English language learners.* (PDF document). Retrieved from http://www.corestandards.org/assets/application-for-english -learners.pdf

Common Core State Standards Initiative (CCSSI). (2010b, June). *Common core state standards: Application to students with disabilities.* (PDF document). Retrieved from http://www. corestandards.org/assets/application-to-students-with -disabilities.pdf

Common Core State Standards Initiative (CCSSI). (2010c, June). *Common core state standards for English language arts and literacy in history/social studies, science, and technical subjects.* (PDF document). Retrieved from http://www.corestandards.org/ assets/CCSSI_ELA%20Standards.pdf

Hattie, J. (2009). *Visible learning: A synthesis of over 800 meta-analyses relating to achievement.* New York, NY: Routledge.

Kelley, J. G., Lesaux, N. K., Kieffer, M. J., & Faller, S. E. (2010). Effective academic vocabulary instruction in the urban middle school. *The Reading Teacher, 64*(1), 5–14.

Lee, C. D., & Spratley, A. (2010). *Reading in the disciplines: The challenges of adolescent literacy.* New York, NY: Carnegie Corporation.

Marzano, R. J. (2004). *Building background knowledge for academic achievement: Research on what works in schools.* Alexandria, VA: Association for Supervision and Curriculum Development.

Nagy, W., & Townsend, D. (2012, January). Words as tools: Vocabulary as language acquisition. *Reading Research Quarterly, 47*(1), 91–108.

Paynter, D. E., Bodrova, E., & Doty, J. K. (2005). *For the love of words: Vocabulary instruction that works.* San Francisco, CA: Jossey-Bass.

Peery, A. (2011). So much more than grammar—How the language strand of the common core state standards supports and strengthens the other strands. In M. A. Wiggs (Ed.), *Navigating the English language arts common core state standards*. Englewood, CO: Lead + Learn Press.

Purves, A. C. (1990). *The scribal society: An essay on literacy in the technological age*. White Plains, NY: Longman.

Scott, J. A., Jamieson-Noel, D., & Asselin, M. (2003, January). Vocabulary instruction throughout the day in twenty-three Canadian upper-elementary classrooms. *The Elementary School Journal, 103*(3), 269–286.

Shanahan, T., & Shanahan, C. (2008, Spring). Teaching disciplinary literacy to adolescents: Rethinking content area literacy. *Harvard Educational Review, 78*(1), 40–59.

Silver, H. F., Dewing, R. T., & Perini, M. J. (2012). *The core six: Essential strategies for achieving with the common core*. Alexandria, VA: ASCD.

Snow, C. E., Lawrence, J. F., & White, C. (2009). Generating knowledge of academic language among urban middle school students. *Journal of Research in Educational Effectiveness, 2*, 325–344.

Stahl, S. A., & Fairbanks, M. M. (1986, Spring). The effects of vocabulary instruction: A model-based meta-analysis. *Review of Educational Research, 56*(1), 72–110.

Vadasy, P. F., & Nelson, J. R. (2012). *What words for special-needs learners: Vocabulary instruction for struggling students*. New York, NY: Guilford.

Watts, S. M. (1995). Vocabulary instruction during reading lessons in six classrooms. *Journal of Reading Behavior, 27*(3), 399–424.

CHAPTER FIVE

Differentiated Instruction in the Secondary School Setting

Thomas Hierck

Secondary schools operate in a much different fashion than their elementary counterparts. Perhaps the biggest difference lies in the scheduling of courses. Whereas most elementary students spend their entire day with the same teacher, secondary students shift by block to different teachers. While elementary students focus on concepts or big ideas, secondary students focus on content. Two themes consistently emerge in the education of adolescent students that seem to suggest that hope for a breakthrough is impossible. The first of these is the notion that the demands of the aforementioned content preclude there being any time left for anything other than standards and high-stakes tests. Class discussion and engaging activities cannot be shoehorned into the "not enough time to cover the course" that is available to teachers. The second notion stems from the rotating schedule mentioned above. Since students switch classes at the end of each period, and there are as many as seven periods a day in some schools, there are too many students for a teacher to get to know. The belief that adolescents are indifferent, sullen, or "too cool for school" further compounds the problem.

A potential solution for schools is to examine their schedules and see where time for collaboration (teacher time to address formative assessment data) and intervention (teacher-student time to address gaps in learning or provide enrichment) can be found. Taken as fact, these two notions might result in educators looking at the Common Core as another burden that the secondary environment simply can't accommodate. Or at the very least, they can't accommodate it for those students identified as "at-risk" or "struggling."

The mission statement for the CCSS is to "provide a consistent, clear understanding of what students are expected to learn, so teachers and parents know what they need to do to help them. The standards are designed to be robust and relevant to the real world, reflecting the knowledge and skills that our young people need for success in college and careers" (CCSSI, 2010). These standards are intended to promote success for all students, including those who might be identified as struggling.

Foushée and Sleigh (2004), in an article for the American Psychological Society, define struggling students as "those who attend class regularly (and appear to be trying) but display poor performance on class assignments and exams; those who perform inconsistently; those who appear less than fully engaged in course activities; and those who have life circumstances impeding progress" (p. 303). Our secondary schools include many students who might fit this definition and the challenge for their teachers is to identify these students as early as possible and begin the process of altering the outcomes for them.

As educators contemplate lesson design and instructional delivery for secondary school students who exhibit some struggles, it may be helpful to ground our thinking on differentiation. A simple definition would include all of the teaching materials and assessment measures that teachers use in providing students with multiple avenues to acquire content and make sense of concepts. Carol Ann Tomlinson (2008) offers a key consideration regardless of where each of our students starts when she says, "What we teach must engage learners or we've lost them before we've begun" (p. 27). Differentiating instruction is part of universal instruction that makes sense for all students as they interact with the content at different levels of understanding and aptitude. Tomlinson (2008) further states that "differentiation calls on teachers to vigilantly monitor student proximity to content goals throughout a learning cycle" (p. 27).

MAKING THE CASE

Traditionally, the difficulties and circumstances mentioned previously have been used as an excuse to explain a lack of student progress or achievement. Laments about students' socioeconomic status, single-parent homes, English language learner status, or native status have been presented to explain student failure. This is despite the lack of any research that would indicate that these circumstances should be viewed as anything other than variables when planning out appropriate interventions or differentiation of instruction. Reeves (2003), in his defining work with 90/90/90 schools (90 percent of students eligible for free or reduced lunch, 90 percent of students from ethnic minority groups, and 90 percent of students meeting the state or district standard in reading or another subject) states that "while economic deprivation clearly affects student achievement, demographic characteristics do not determine academic performance" (p. 1).

Researchers Lacour and Tissington (2011) point out that "instructional techniques and strategies implemented at the classroom, school, district, and government levels can help close the achievement gap by providing students with necessary assistance in order to achieve high performance in academics" (p. 527). Their study looked at the impact of poverty on student achievement, but the same analysis can be applied to any of the other circumstances that might be presented as a rationale for a lack of achievement. When viewed as variables requiring a different approach by teachers, these challenges can be overcome. As students complete their time in school and enter the next phase of their lives (whether post-secondary studies or careers), it is essential that they are fluent in those skills required for them to flourish in the 21st century. A focus on creativity and innovation, critical thinking and problem solving, communication, and collaboration is essential to prepare students for the future they will enter. The Partnership for 21st Century Skills has created a planning template for schools to use in their design of lessons and instructional planning (see the Resources section at the end of this chapter).

What then of the notion often heard at schools that "all students can learn"? Can we move beyond the trite phrase to a belief that can be actualized, or will we continue to think "all students can learn except..."? Buffum, Mattos, and Weber (2012) provide this clarity when talking about all students: "All includes any student who will be expected to live as a financially independent adult someday" (p. 19). They go on to suggest that if this is our target group, then we need to ensure high school graduation plus further training or studies. Hence one of the strong underpinnings of the Common Core—all students must be prepared to compete with not only their peers in the next district, but with students from around the world. Having standards that are aligned with college or work expectations and that are internationally benchmarked will allow for all students to be prepared to succeed in the global economy and society.

With this imperative as the backdrop, what initiatives exist for secondary schools to move to this view of maximum levels of achievement for the vast majority of students? What differentiation strategies are available that don't seem to be adding more to an already overflowing plate of expectations for teachers? The solution lies in our approach to providing the high-quality instruction necessary for kids to succeed.

Effective teachers have differentiated long before the label came along. Tomlinson (1999) talks about differentiation in terms of the actions taken by teachers. She says these teachers "accept, embrace, and plan for the fact that learners bring many commonalities to school, but that learners also bring the essential differences that make them individuals" (p. 2). The differentiating teacher plans instruction so that it is a good fit for each individual. Tomlinson (2003) addresses this notion. "To teach each student from his or her point of entry into the curriculum and perspective as a learner is more than difficult. It is a goal beyond the grasp of even the most expert teacher. The outcome for students who are outliers, however, is likely to be vastly different when a teacher pursues that elusive goal than when the teacher—by intent or default—abandons it" (p. 7).

The likelihood that this level of differentiation can occur in conjunction with a drive to cover all of the standards that are part of today's courses is slim. To address that, another action needs to be taken by educators—the identification of Priority Standards. Ainsworth (2010) states, "Priority Standards provide educators with a sharp and consistent focus for in-depth instruction and related assessment. They provide students with multiple opportunities to learn those standards as opposed to one-time instructional exposure to them" (p. 40). Reeves (2001) speaks to this notion more specifically through the lens of the struggling student: "Because of the limitations of time and the extraordinary variety in learning backgrounds of students, teachers and leaders need focus and clarity in order to prepare their students for success" (p. 167). As a result of the two factors that Reeves cites, the interventions utilized at the secondary level need to be more specific than at the elementary level. The following sections address specific ways to differentiate for secondary students.

WHAT WORKS IN
THE SECONDARY SETTING?

Much success in the secondary setting lies in approaches built off the work of Benjamin Bloom (mastery learning), John Hattie (direct instruction), and the Response to Intervention (RTI) approach.

Bloom's mastery learning approach centered on teachers doing the following to achieve mastery learning (Guskey and Jung, 2011):

• Organize the important concepts into instructional units.

• Follow with high-quality initial instruction.

• Administer a *formative* assessment that provides feedback to teachers and students on learning progress.

- Suggest corrective activities that are specific to items or prompts within the assessment so that students can work on those particular concepts they have not yet mastered.
- Administer a second, parallel, formative assessment after students have completed their corrective activities.

Bloom believed that nearly all students instructed using the mastery learning approach could master academic content. The research is strongly in support of this assertion. Comparisons with students in traditionally taught classes suggest that students in classes taught through mastery learning have higher levels of achievement (Anderson, 1994; Guskey and Pigott, 1988; Kulik, Kulik, and Bangert-Drowns, 1990). Additionally, they "develop greater confidence in their ability to learn and in themselves as learners" (Guskey and Jung, 2011, p. 251). Guskey (2010) has suggested, "If teachers could provide the necessary time and appropriate learning conditions, nearly all students could reach a high level of achievement" (p. 52). Indeed, the 90/90/90 schools cited earlier all employed the Data Teams process, a process that identifies students meeting or exceeding a standard, those who are close to meeting it, those who are further away, and those who need intensive assistance. This process has led to high achievement in many schools and bears similarities to the mastery learning approach.

Hattie's (2009) research suggests that direct instruction is effective for all students and across all subjects. His meta-analyses of 800 studies concludes that "experienced experts possess pedagogical content knowledge that is more flexibly and innovatively employed in instruction; they are more able to improvise and alter instruction in response to the contextual features of the classroom situation; they understand at a deeper level the reasons for individual student success and failure on any given academic task; their understanding of students is such that they are more able to provide developmentally appropriate learning tasks that engage, challenge, and even intrigue students..." (p. 261).

Hattie is quick to clarify that direct instruction should not be confused with the "stand and deliver" approach that critics often misinterpret it as being. Instead, direct instruction can be clarified as an approach where:

> The teacher decides the learning intentions and success criteria, makes them transparent to the students, demonstrates them by modeling, evaluates if they understand what they have been told by checking for understanding, and retell[s] them what they have [been] told by tying it all together with closure. (p. 206)

These steps define a clear approach to differentiating instruction that ensures all students can access the content at their current level of understanding.

The essential components of an RTI system include the following (National Association of State Directors of Special Education, 2005):

- High-quality instruction and learning opportunities matched to students' needs

- Identification of students struggling to meet grade-level expectations

- Attention to students' learning rates and levels of performance

- Increasing intensity of instruction/intervention based on students' needs

• Data-informed educational decisions using a team problem-solving method

Implementation of the essential components of RTI (screening, progress monitoring, data-based decision making, and a multilevel prevention system) provides schools with an approach to master the key expectations of the Common Core. The goal of RTI is to help every student access the grade-level standards in a very strong and effective core instructional program that is standards-based, data-driven, and responsive to student needs. Effective use of data from multiple assessment measures lets teachers make good decisions about what they are teaching so that they don't necessarily teach students what they already know, but really focus on the things they don't know, and identify where those gaps or holes are.

Some researchers have suggested that "high school completion data indicate that passing grade 9 algebra and English classes places students on a positive trajectory and that not passing these classes is significantly correlated with dropping out" (National High School Center, National Center on Response to Intervention, and Center on Instruction, 2010, p. 2). Recent data downloaded from Statistic Brain (2013) suggests that over a third (36 percent) of dropouts occur in the ninth grade and that students who repeat this grade only have a 15 percent graduation rate. Clearly this critical factor needs to be considered as we design our interventions with an eye toward the graduation potential of students in high school. Two models that have been shown to be effective and deserve further consideration involve additional time for students struggling in these key academic areas. The first model involves scheduling an additional block of time as part of a student's course requirements. In this approach each student would get the equivalent of a block and a half in the key academic area. The additional hours of instruction would allow students to close the gap and prevent further learning loss. The second approach involves a shorter chunk of time. In this approach a student would be pulled from another content area to receive additional time to address the learning deficit. Both these models stir up emotions as educators wonder about the missed content areas that get sacrificed in order for the student to receive the additional time. The corollary to these concerns, as legitimate as they are, was outlined in the first few sentences of this paragraph— students who struggle in these key academic areas struggle everywhere, and do not have high success rates. It is imperative that we do something to reverse the trend.

My colleague Chris Weber developed Exhibit 5.1 to help school teams focus their collaboration time on the key aspects of RTI. This planning template may be a good starting point for discussing differentiation and intervention at your school.

When looking at what aspects of RTI might be most effective for secondary students, it is important to consider that implementing tiered interventions at the high school level involves more than the "cutting and pasting" of the essential components of RTI from elementary schools. A number of factors exist that drive the design, delivery, and assessment for struggling students at the secondary level. Exhibit 5.2 was adapted from the High School Tiered Interventions Initiative (HSTII) team that produced a report for the National High School Center (2010). It outlines some of the considerations secondary schools should keep paramount.

BOOK FIVE EXHIBIT 5.1

Five RTI Questions for Collaborative Teams

RTI Questions				
1. Which students do we have concerns about?				
2. In what areas do we have concerns? a. Academics b. Academic behaviors c. Social behaviors				
3. What are we currently doing to support the student and meet the student's needs?				
4. What supports will we be providing in the future?				
5. Has the student responded to the instruction and interventions we have been providing?				

Key Considerations and Questions for Secondary Schools

Focus: Each school needs to determine its purpose and scope of tiered interventions, keeping in mind that no standard application of the framework exists at the high school level.	• What will be the purpose and scope of tiered interventions in our school? • How will existing initiatives fit into the tiered interventions framework? • How will we align current special education and instructional support practices with tiered interventions? • Will other initiatives hinder the implementation of tiered interventions?
Culture: A school's culture provides both formal and informal guidance for decisions made within the organization. Staff members could collaborate in new ways, examine data together regularly, and think about implications for instructional practice.	• In what ways will current practices, beliefs, and behaviors align with the goals and purposes for our tiered intervention framework? • What changes might be required for staff to collaborate, examine student data, and act on what they learn from the data?

Instructional Organization: The instructional organization of high school can create challenges and require flexibility in the scheduling and delivery of interventions for students and collaborative time for teachers.	• How will the staff create and/or adapt a master schedule that allows:
	
	  • Student access to tiered supports
	  • Time for teachers to collaborate
	  • Time for teachers to discuss data
	  • Movement between tiers for students

Continued

BOOK FIVE EXHIBIT 5.2

Key Considerations and Questions for Secondary Schools (Continued)

Staff Roles: High school teachers often view themselves as teachers of content and not necessarily equipped to teach struggling students, students with disabilities, and/or English language learners. Small schools may have less access to instructional specialists. Staff expertise and school priorities help to determine which approach will be implemented.	• If tiered interventions are implemented in more than one content area, how will we support content teachers in becoming more than "teachers of content"?
Student Involvement: High school students could help select appropriate interventions and monitor their progress, resulting in students feeling more involved in their educational experience.	• How will students be involved in the monitoring of their progress? • What role will students play in determining movement between tiers?
Implementation and Alignment: It is critical to align efforts that can support and accelerate the implementation of tiered interventions. A detailed scaling-up plan may be useful for incrementally expanding the focus and scope of the framework.	• What options will exist for scaling up the implementation of tiered interventions over time to broaden the number of students, content areas, and/or interventions?
Instruction and Assessment Resources: Few measures appropriate for screening or progress-monitoring purposes have been validated for use with high school students.	• How will school leaders select interventions? • What data will support the use of particular interventions in high school?

Source: Adapted from National High School Center, National Center on Response to Intervention, and Center on Instruction, 2010.

ACADEMICS OR BEHAVIOR?
FOCUS ON BOTH

Read these two scenarios. Which school would you rather attend if you were a student?

Scenario 1: In our school, we implement a systematic approach to intervention to guarantee that *all* students will learn the essential grade-level learning outcomes and to guarantee that we, the educators in the building, will know when the essential learning outcomes are learned and what to do for each individual student if learning has not occurred. This requires regular Professional Learning Community meetings approximately every three to five weeks for 30 to 45 minutes. We will screen *all* new students to determine who needs immediate intervention in the first two weeks of the school year and to determine program placement. (Are the right students enrolled in our support classes? Have we missed anyone? Do we need to move anyone?) We will build flextime into the schedule to allow for intervention time without pulling students out of core classes. Our approach is consistent for behavior and academics and our early screening attempts to identify any potential issues so we can plan for interventions immediately.

Scenario 2: We believe in a "wait until they fail" model, where students receive intervention after their struggles have resulted in a lack of progress and they have become behavioral challenges for us to manage. That way we can remove them from school. Our collaboration time is really our only chance to catch up on our grading of papers. We trust that our special education department can handle the variety of referrals we send their way. Our administrators will handle all of the behavioral concerns as we focus on the academic rigor in classrooms.

Of course the question is rhetorical, as no educator would think that the second option would produce the best outcomes for students. (I am grateful to principal Charlie Coleman and members of his school team at Cowichan Secondary School for sharing some of their year-opening procedures outlined in scenario 1.) And yet, many schools still operate on the notion that behavior and academics are separate entities with little overlap. This belief persists despite research (Hawkins, Catalano, Kosterman, Abbott, and Hill, 1999) that shows that when schools work to decrease behavior problems, academic achievement improves. Recent authors (Buffum, Mattos, and Weber, 2009; Hierck, Coleman, and Weber, 2011) posit that academics and behavior are inextricably linked. It just makes sense that less time spent on behavioral challenges leads to more on-task time and, as Guskey (2010) alluded to, this additional time is a key component to learning for all. The research clearly shows that more instructional time is highly correlated with student achievement (Brophy, 1988; Fisher, Berliner, Filby, Marliave, Cahen, and Dishaw, 1980). In a study that looked at office discipline referrals and suspensions, Scott and Barrett (2004) estimate that when a student receives an office discipline referral he/she loses twenty minutes of instructional time, and when a student is given a suspension he/she loses one day of instructional time. For our struggling learners, this serves the purpose of compounding existing gaps in their learning, making success an even less likely outcome.

Studies at the secondary level that examined the relationship between academic performance and problem behaviors yield further support for the behavior-academics connection. Tobin and Sugai (1999) showed that academic failure in high school was linked to students receiving three or more suspensions in ninth grade. Morrison, Anthony, Storino, and Dillon (2001) analyzed the records of students who received in-school suspensions. Those students who did not receive an in-school suspension had higher grade point averages than the students who had. Roeser, Eccles, and Sameroff (2000) examined the connection between problem behavior and academic performance and found that the relationship strengthens over the time spent in middle school. These findings demonstrate that higher rates of office discipline referrals and suspensions are correlated with lower scores on academic assessments in the upper grades.

Let's be crystal clear here: differentiation is about our approach to all aspects of a student's school life—academics, behaviors, and academic behaviors. As Buffum, Mattos, and Weber (2009) suggest when talking about the high levels of success that occurred at Glen Levey Middle School under the leadership of principal Anthony Muhammad, "Until the school created a safe, orderly campus that addressed students' social and emotional needs, it could not address their academic needs" (p. 122). Educators need to adopt a structure for dealing with behavioral deficits that is similar to the instructional structure used to deal with academic deficits, rather than quickly resorting to consequences that include removal from the academic environment that struggling students need to spend more time immersed in, not less. Teachers do not expect that students will know all of the academic content of their grade or course and anticipate where the struggles might be. They go further by building alternate formats for presenting the content to struggling students and reteaching when necessary. A similar expectation should be anticipated in the realm of behavior. Not all students will know all of the expected behavior for a grade or course. Rather than sentencing a student to special education (from which that student will usually never return if the behavior is severe) or utilizing suspension too frequently, schools and districts need to engage in planning and design that allows for a differentiated approach to students reaching desired behavior goals. This is not to suggest that consequences should never occur, but rather that the extreme form of consequence outlined above should be reserved for the smallest percentage of students for which a well-defined and clearly articulated differentiation model has not achieved the desired outcomes.

MOTIVATION AND ENGAGEMENT

Students come to our schools with different interests, experiences, maturity levels, prior knowledge, and abilities. As a result, teachers are regularly challenged to come up with differentiated instructional strategies matching the gifts students possess. This is not to suggest that teachers need a strategy for each student; instead, teachers need a variety of teaching and assessing methods that serve to engage students and provide the necessary motivation for them to achieve at their highest levels.

When focused on struggling learners, the challenge becomes magnified, as their individual success will be contingent on positive learning experiences that match the skills they currently possess. All students, but especially struggling students, need to see value in what they are learning. They need to see a connection to their learning and feel they have some control over the learning process. Glaze and Mattingley (2008) suggest, "Students are more likely to concentrate and make an effort when their schoolwork is personally meaningful and engaging" (p. 22).

What can we do to motivate our struggling learners? Here are some practices that have proven to be effective:

1. Build in opportunities for social interaction. A student may find an otherwise boring or frustrating task to be more motivating if the activity provides an opportunity for social interaction. Various cooperative learning strategies, like reciprocal teaching and jigsaw, provide this much-needed social interaction.

2. Provide an authentic audience for student work. For example, teachers could encourage students to submit their work to publications, post it on Web sites, or present it to in-school audiences.

3. Connect academic assignments to real-world situations. When students see that content covered in their coursework can help to explain how actual problems were created or solved, they can sense the real power of academic knowledge and its potential to affect human lives.

4. Offer students meaningful choices whenever possible. When students are offered some degree of autonomy and choice in selecting or carrying out an activity, they are more motivated to take part in that activity. Let students choose paper and project topics that interest them. Assess them in a variety of ways (tests, papers, projects, presentations) to give students more control over how they show their understanding.

5. Make learning fun. Use game formats—Jeopardy!-style activities, for example—to liven up academic material and engage student interest.

The key to any breakthrough is to connect the instructional strategy to the need of the students. There won't be a "one size fits all" approach that will unlock the learning for all struggling students, but we can increase the likelihood of success for those students by discovering the key to their learning preferences. Research shows that a lack of student engagement is predictive of dropping out even after controlling for academic achievement and student background. Both academic and social engagement are integral components of successfully navigating the education pipeline (Rumberger, 2004).

Phillip Schlechty (2009) states that "engagement results when students are attentive, persistent, and committed. Students value and find meaning in the work and learn what they are expected to learn" (p. 1). He identifies five different levels of engagement as outlined in Exhibit 5.3, based on the decisions students make regarding the personal consequences of doing a task or participating in an activity. His model clearly indicates that personal meaning is a vital component of engagement and that as this wanes, students move away from being attentive or even compliant to being outright rebellious and withdrawn. Academic routines that are engaging and meaningful and behavior that is appropriate and appreciated are inextricably linked. In Schlechty's view, the priority for the teacher is to "design engaging tasks and activities for students that call upon students to learn what the school has determined they should learn and then to lead students to success in completion of these tasks" (p. 3).

Schlechty's Levels of Engagement

	Attention	Compliance	Commitment
Authentic Engagement	High	Yes	High
Strategic Compliance	High	Yes	Low
Passive (Ritual) Compliance	Low	Yes	Low
Retreat	No	Yes	No
Rebellion	No	No	No

Source: Adapted from Schlechty, 2009.

Schlechty goes on to describe three types of classrooms with varying degrees of student engagement. The engaged classroom features students authentically engaged most or some of the time.
The compliant classroom features ritual engagement and passive
compliance. There is the mistaken belief that effective learning is
taking place, but this should not be confused with authentic engagement. The off-task classroom tends to be distinguished by
patterns of rebellion and retreatism. While occasional moments

of authentic and ritual engagement may occur, teachers in this type of classroom get preoccupied with trying to manage students rather than leading their acquisition of knowledge, which would ultimately lead to authentic engagement. In a differentiated approach, teachers focus on the engagement of all students and meet them where their needs are.

SUMMARY

The differences in schooling that students can expect when they move from the elementary to the secondary school setting (largely timetabling and course expectations) can be mitigated by educators who focus on collaboration and taking a differentiated approach to ensure learning for all. The Common Core State Standards invite a fresh look at what can be done to ensure our struggling students are engaged in relevant and meaningful tasks that offer the potential to close the gaps in their learning and put them on a course for success in the transition to college or a career.

The implementation of the Common Core will bring further changes to a constantly evolving school system. As evidenced in the introductory statements about the changes, "These Standards are not intended to be new names for old ways of doing business. They are a call to take the next step. It is time for states to work together to build on lessons learned from two decades of standards-based reforms. It is time to recognize that these standards are not just promises to our children, but promises we intend to keep" (CCSSI, 2010).

Why is this so important, and in particular why is it so important for our struggling students? In the United States, approximately 7,000 students drop out every school day (Alliance for Excellent Education, n.d.). In bygone days this may not have been a significant factor in their lives, since a high school dropout could earn a living wage. That era has ended in the United States. In the 21st century, dropping out significantly diminishes people's chances to secure good jobs and promising futures. This is compounded even further when one considers the substantial financial and social costs to their communities, states, and the country in which they live. One startling statistic should solidify the importance of reversing the trend for struggling students and working to improve their life chances. The Alliance for Excellent Education estimates (2006) that "increasing the graduation rate and college matriculation of male students in the United States by just five percent could lead to combined savings and revenue of almost $8 billion each year by reducing crime-related costs" (p. 1).

Teachers are in the best position to create a differentiated environment that enriches the life of each student. In this environment, students gain the ability to close the gaps in their academic learning and acquire appropriate behaviors. They are able to work through the challenges and are strengthened because of their progression through those difficult situations. Teachers have an indispensable role to play in generating this differentiated environment. To do otherwise ensures that the startling statistics shared earlier become a reality for far too many of our students.

Let's turn to Tomlinson (2003) for one final thought: "Ultimately, just one question might best serve diverse learners, their teachers, and their society. What can we do to support educators in developing the skill and the will to teach for each learner's equity of access to excellence?" (p. 11).

RESOURCES

THE PARTNERSHIP FOR 21ST-CENTURY SKILLS PLANNING TEMPLATE

Learning and Innovation Skills

Learning and innovation skills increasingly are being recognized as those that separate students who are prepared for increasingly complex life and work environments in the 21st century, and those who are not. A focus on creativity and innovation, critical thinking and problem solving, and communication and collaboration is essential to prepare students for the future:

Creativity and Innovation

- Think creatively
  - Use a wide range of idea creation techniques (such as brainstorming)
  - Create new and worthwhile ideas (both incremental and radical concepts)
  - Elaborate, refine, analyze, and evaluate one's own ideas in order to improve and maximize creative effort
- Work creatively with others
  - Develop, implement, and communicate new ideas to others effectively
  - Be open and responsive to new and diverse perspectives; incorporate group input and feedback into the work
  - Demonstrate originality and inventiveness in work and understand the real-world limits to adopting new ideas
  - View failure as an opportunity to learn; understand that creativity and innovation is a long-term, cyclical process of small successes and frequent mistakes

- Implement Innovations
  - Act on creative ideas to make a tangible, useful contribution to the field in which the innovation will occur

How is your school ensuring that all students master creativity and innovation?

Critical Thinking and Problem Solving

- Reason effectively
  - Use various types of reasoning (inductive, deductive, etc.) as appropriate to the situation
- Use systems thinking
  - Analyze how parts of a whole interact with each other to produce overall outcomes in complex systems
- Make judgments and decisions
  - Effectively analyze and evaluate evidence, arguments, claims, and beliefs
  - Analyze and evaluate major alternative points of view
  - Synthesize and make connections between information and arguments
  - Interpret information and draw conclusions based on the best analysis
  - Reflect critically on learning experiences and processes

- Solve problems
  - Solve different kinds of unfamiliar problems in both conventional and innovative ways
  - Identify and ask significant questions that clarify various points of view and lead to better solutions

How is your school ensuring that all students master critical thinking and problem solving?

Communication and Collaboration

- Communicate clearly
  - Articulate thoughts and ideas effectively using oral, written, and nonverbal communication skills in a variety of forms and contexts
  - Listen effectively to decipher meaning, including knowledge, values, attitudes, and intentions
  - Use communication for a range of purposes (e.g., to inform, instruct, motivate, and persuade)
  - Utilize multiple media and technologies, and know how to judge their effectiveness a priori as well as assess their impact
  - Communicate effectively in diverse environments (including multilingual)
- Collaborate with others
  - Demonstrate ability to work effectively and respectfully with diverse teams

- Exercise flexibility and willingness to be helpful in making necessary compromises to accomplish a common goal
- Assume shared responsibility for collaborative work, and value the individual contributions made by each team member

How is your school ensuring that all students master communication and collaboration?

Information, Media, and Technology Skills

People in the 21st century live in a technology- and media-suffused environment, marked by various characteristics, including: 1) access to an abundance of information, 2) rapid changes in technology tools, and 3) the ability to collaborate and make individual contributions on an unprecedented scale. To be effective in the 21st century, citizens and workers must be able to exhibit a range of functional and critical thinking skills related to information, media, and technology.

Information Literacy

- Access and evaluate information
  - Access information efficiently (time) and effectively (sources)
  - Evaluate information critically and competently

- Use and manage information
  - Use information accurately and creatively for the issue or problem at hand
  - Manage the flow of information from a wide variety of sources
  - Apply a fundamental understanding of the ethical/legal issues surrounding the access and use of information

Media Literacy

- Analyze media
  - Understand both how and why media messages are constructed, and for what purposes
  - Examine how individuals interpret messages differently, how values and points of view are included or excluded, and how media can influence beliefs and behaviors
  - Apply a fundamental understanding of the ethical/legal issues surrounding the access and use of media
- Create media products
  - Understand and utilize the most appropriate media creation tools, characteristics, and conventions
  - Understand and effectively utilize the most appropriate expressions and interpretations in diverse, multicultural environments

ICT (Information, Communications, and Technology) Literacy

- Apply technology effectively
  - Use technology as a tool to research, organize, evaluate, and communicate information
  - Use digital technologies (computers, PDAs, media players, GPS, etc.), communication/networking tools, and social networks appropriately to access, manage, integrate, evaluate, and create information to successfully function in a knowledge economy
  - Apply a fundamental understanding of the ethical/legal issues surrounding the access and use of information technologies

How is your school ensuring that all students master information, media, and technology skills?

Life and Career Skills

Today's life and work environments require far more than thinking skills and content knowledge. The ability to navigate the complex life and work environments in the globally competitive information age requires students to pay rigorous attention to developing adequate life and career skills.

Flexibility and Adaptability

- Adapt to change
    - Adapt to varied roles, jobs responsibilities, schedules, and contexts
    - Work effectively in a climate of ambiguity and changing priorities
- Be flexible
    - Incorporate feedback effectively
    - Deal positively with praise, setbacks, and criticism
    - Understand, negotiate, and balance diverse views and beliefs to reach workable solutions, particularly in multicultural environments

Initiative and Self-Direction

- Manage goals and time
  - Set goals with tangible and intangible success criteria
  - Balance tactical (short-term) and strategic (long-term) goals
  - Utilize time and manage workload efficiently
- Work independently
  - Monitor, define, prioritize, and complete tasks without direct oversight
- Be self-directed learners
  - Go beyond basic mastery of skills and/or curriculum to explore and expand one's own learning and opportunities to gain expertise
  - Demonstrate initiative to advance skill levels toward a professional level
  - Demonstrate commitment to learning as a lifelong process
  - Reflect critically on past experiences in order to inform future progress

Social and Cross-Cultural Skills

- Interact effectively with others
  - Know when it is appropriate to listen and when to speak
  - Conduct oneself in a respectable, professional manner
- Work effectively in diverse teams
  - Respect cultural differences and work effectively with people from a range of social and cultural backgrounds
  - Respond open-mindedly to different ideas and values
  - Leverage social and cultural differences to create new ideas and increase both innovation and quality of work

Productivity and Accountability

- Manage projects
  - Set and meet goals, even in the face of obstacles and competing pressures

- Prioritize, plan, and manage work to achieve the intended result
- Produce results
  - Demonstrate additional attributes associated with producing high-quality products including the abilities to:
    - Work positively and ethically
    - Manage time and projects effectively
    - Multi-task
    - Participate actively, as well as be reliable and punctual
    - Present oneself professionally and with proper etiquette
    - Collaborate and cooperate effectively with teams
    - Respect and appreciate team diversity
    - Be accountable for results

Leadership and Responsibility

- Guide and lead others
  - Use interpersonal and problem-solving skills to influence and guide others toward a goal
  - Leverage strengths of others to accomplish a common goal
  - Inspire others to reach their very best via example and selflessness
  - Demonstrate integrity and ethical behavior in using influence and power
- Be responsible to others
  - Act responsibly with the interests of the larger community in mind

How is your school ensuring that all students master life and career skills?

References

Ainsworth, L. (2010). *Rigorous curriculum design.* Englewood, CO: Lead + Learn Press.

Alliance for Excellent Education. (n.d.). *The crisis in American high schools.* Washington: Author. Retrieved from http://www.all4ed.org/whats_at_stake/CrisisInHighSchools.pdf

Alliance for Excellent Education. (2006). *Saving futures, saving dollars: The impact of education on crime reduction and earnings.* Retrieved from http://www.all4ed.org/files/SavingFutures.pdf

Anderson, S. A. (1994). *Synthesis of research on mastery learning.* Washington, DC: National Education Association. ERIC Document Reproduction Service No. ED 382 567.

Brophy, J. E. (1988). Research linking teacher behavior to student achievement: Potential implications for instruction of chapter 1 students. *Educational Psychologist, 23,* 235–286.

Buffum, A., Mattos, M., & Weber, C. (2009). *Pyramid response to intervention: RTI, professional learning communities, and how to respond when kids don't learn.* Bloomington, IN: Solution Tree.

Buffum, A., Mattos, M., & Weber, C. (2012). *Simplifying response to intervention: Four essential guiding principles.* Bloomington, IN: Solution Tree.

Common Core State Standards Initiative (CCSSI). (2010). *Common core state standards.* Retrieved from www.corestandards.org

Fisher, C. W., Berliner, D. C., Filby, N. N., Marliave, R., Cahen, L. S., & Dishaw, M. M. (1980). Teaching behaviors, academic learning time, and student achievement: An overview. *Journal of Classroom Interaction, 17*(1), 2–15.

Foushée, R. D., & Sleigh, M. J. (2004). Going the extra mile: Identifying and assisting struggling students. In B. Perlman, L. I. McCann, & S. H. McFadden (Eds.), *Lessons learned: Practical advice for the teaching of psychology* (vol. 2, pp. 303–311). Washington, DC: American Psychological Society.

Glaze, A., & Mattingley, R. (2008). *Class interrupted: Strategies for positive behaviour (classroom focus).* Edmonton, Alberta, Canada: Pearson.

Gregg, L. A. (2012). *Response to instructional strategies and interventions.* Englewood, CO: Lead + Learn Press.

Guskey, T. R. (2010). Mastery learning. *Educational Leadership, 68*(2), 53–57.

Guskey, T. R., & Jung, L. A. (2011). Response-to-intervention and mastery learning: Tracing roots and seeking common ground. *The Clearing House: A Journal of Educational Strategies, Issues and Ideas, 84*(6), 249–255.

Guskey, T. R., & Pigott, T. D. (1988). Research on group-based mastery learning programs: A meta-analysis. *Journal of Educational Research, 81,* 197–216.

Hattie, J. (2009). *Visible learning: A synthesis of over 800 meta-analyses relating to student achievement.* New York, NY: Routledge.

Hawkins, J. D., Catalano, R. F., Kosterman, R., Abbott, R., & Hill, K. G. (1999). Preventing adolescent health-risk behaviors by strengthening protection during childhood. *Archives of Pediatric and Adolescent Medicine, 153,* 226–234.

Hierck, T., Coleman, C., & Weber, C. (2011). *Pyramid of behavior interventions: 7 keys to a positive learning environment.* Bloomington, IN: Solution Tree.

Kulik, C. C., Kulik, J. A., & Bangert-Drowns, R. L. (1990). Effectiveness of mastery learning programs: A meta-analysis. *Review of Educational Research 60,* 265–99.

Lacour, M., & Tissington, L. D. (2011). The effects of poverty on academic achievement. *Educational Research and Reviews, 6*(7), 522–527.

Morrison, G. M., Anthony, S., Storino, M., & Dillon, C. (2001). An examination of the disciplinary histories and the individual and educational characteristics of students who participate in an in-school suspension program. *Education and Treatment of Children, 24*, 276–293.

National Association of State Directors of Special Education. (2005). *Response to intervention: Policy considerations and implementation.* Retrieved from www.nasdse.org

National High School Center, National Center on Response to Intervention, and Center on Instruction. (2010). *Tiered interventions in high schools: Using preliminary "lessons learned" to guide ongoing discussion.* Washington, DC: American Institutes for Research.

Partnership for 21st Century Skills. (2011). *Planning template.* Retrieved from www.p21.org

Reeves, D. B. (2001). *101 questions & answers about standards, assessment, and accountability.* Englewood, CO: Advanced Learning Press.

Reeves, D. (2003). *High performance in high poverty schools: 90/90/90 and beyond.* Center for Performance Assessment.

Roeser, R. W., Eccles, J. S., & Sameroff, A. J. (2000). School as a context of early adolescents' academic and social-emotional development: A summary of research findings. *The Elementary School Journal, 100*(5), 443–471.

Rumberger, R. (2004). Why students drop out of school. In G. Orfield (Ed.), *Dropouts in America: Confronting the graduation rate crisis* (pp. 131–155). Cambridge, MA: Harvard Education Press.

Schlechty, P. (2009). *Schlechty Center on engagement.* Retrieved from http://www.schlechtycenter.org/tools/free

Scott, T. M., & Barrett, S. B. (2004). Using staff and student time engaged in disciplinary procedures to evaluate the impact of school-wide PBS. *Journal of Positive Behavior Interventions, 6*(1), 21–27.

Statistic Brain. (2013). High school dropout statistics. Retrieved from http://www.statisticbrain.com/high-school-dropout-statistics/

Tobin, T., & Sugai, G. (1999). Predicting violence at school, chronic discipline problems, and high school outcomes from sixth graders' school records. *Journal of Emotional Disorders, 7*, 40–53.

Tomlinson, C. A. (1999). *The differentiated classroom: Responding to the needs of all learners.* Alexandria, VA: Association for Supervision and Curriculum Development.

Tomlinson, C. A. (2003). Deciding to teach them all. *Educational Leadership, 61*(2), 6–11.

Tomlinson, C. A. (2008). The goals of differentiation. *Educational Leadership, 66*(3), 26–30.

CHAPTER SIX

Effective Direct Instruction to Support Response to Intervention

Chris Weber

The Common Core State Standards, when "unwrapped" (Ainsworth, 2003) and well understood by educators, are of critical importance. Even more important, however, are the ways in which, and the depth to which, educators help students achieve mastery of the key content. In the last decade of the 20th century and the first decade of the 21st century, American education has been dominated by curriculum, at the expense of a focus on instruction. The quality and research bases of programs may have improved, but an unfortunate consequence of curriculum's elevated position over instruction has been that instruction and lesson design have become a lost art. Prescribed lesson scripts have been trusted to replace teaching; differentiation has been sacrificed in favor of one-size-fits-all approaches (Tomlinson, 2001; Elmore, 2010; Ainsworth, 2013).

Highly effective instruction is critical for all students, but particularly for students at risk. The narratives that support the Common Core State Standards make this remarkably and importantly clear, and outline why and how high-quality instruction is essential to prepare all students for college and career readiness. The most critical tier of Response to Intervention (RTI) is Tier 1, core instruction (Buffum, Mattos, & Weber, 2009). The best intervention is prevention. All students will thrive with better-designed and better-delivered core instruction. For struggling students, effective instruction is a life-saving and life-changing necessity.

Textbooks do not teach students; teachers do. Instruction must be designed and cognitively planned so that teachers clearly define the learning targets that students will be expected to master. Learning must be made relevant, and new learning must be connected to prior knowledge. Teachers must model critical thinking and problem solving and gradually release responsibility to students. Targeted questioning, frequent checks for understanding, and immediate, specific, corrective feedback must guide learning. Students must be assigned differentiated tasks that match their current levels of readiness, and teachers must confer with groups of students to meet their targeted needs. Teachers must close lessons by connecting knowledge to the learning targets and gathering evidence of levels of student mastery.

What's new about effective instruction in the Common Core era? Nothing. The research and practices of effective instruction are as robust and necessary as ever. However, differences may be seen in the depth of understanding required of students and the ways in which that understanding must be demonstrated. Well-designed and well-delivered instruction is now more critical than ever.

Routines, procedures, and structures may be adapted to suit a particular grade level and content area, but the key common elements of effective instruction must always be present.

The purpose of this chapter is three-fold:

- Describe why the elements of effective instruction are necessary and how they interact.

- Provide specific examples of tasks within the elements of effective instruction.

- Combine the attributes of the best thinking around lesson design and delivery that will ensure that all students meet the expectations of the Common Core.

RESEARCH AND MODELS OF EFFECTIVE INSTRUCTION

Effective instruction can be defined. Best practices that result in relatively greater levels of student learning have been validated. Meta-analyses have confirmed the efficacy of direct-instruction models and related elements in promoting high rates of learning.

John Hattie's (2009) comprehensive synthesis of decades of educational research validates the elements of effective instruction that will be described in this chapter. Direct instruction is specifically validated; however, Hattie is careful to distinguish direct instruction from didactic, teacher-led, lecture-based instruction. Hattie's definition of direct instruction includes the following components:

- Clear learning targets

- Clear descriptions of success at meeting targets

- Connections of new learning to existing schema and to real life

- Modeling of new learning with a gradual release of responsibility to students
- Practice of new learning guided by the teacher with frequent checks for understanding and immediate, specific, corrective feedback
- Closure, during which teachers assess the lesson's success
- Independent practice

Hattie, in *Visible Learning* (2009), notes that direct instruction works with all types of learners in all content areas. The critical importance of effective first instruction to RTI cannot be overstated. A common refrain of schools is that they have identified an overwhelming number of students in need of supplemental Tier 2 and Tier 3 supports. When this occurs, the effectiveness of core instruction must be examined as representing one of the first variables we must consider. RTI is perhaps best operationalized as RTI^2, Response to *instruction* and intervention (Buffum, Mattos, & Weber, 2009). We will never "intervene" our way to college and career readiness for all. Core instruction must be continuously analyzed and improved. Furthermore, student learning as a result of direct instruction models is superior to learning that results from other models. Marzano's meta-analyses (Marzano, 2003; Marzano, Pickering, and Pollock, 2001) and Reeves' (2006) studies also validate the elements of direct instruction.

Direct instruction has become a target for the wrath of teachers, but the instruction that Hattie, Marzano, and Reeves cite as effective would not include traits misattributed to direct instruction, such as the following:

- Skill and drill

- Teaching and learning of facts and procedures in isolation from meaningful contexts
- One-size-fits-all teaching
- Rote learning
- An overuse of lecture

Students have been shown to learn more when structures are in place (Black and Wiliam, 1998; Duke and Pearson, 2002; Hattie, 2009; Doyle, 1983; City, Elmore, Fiarman, and Teitel, 2009; Leithwood, Anderson, Mascall, and Strauss, 2010; Marzano, 2003; Newmann and Wehlage, 1993). Too many lessons are unstructured, following the "I do it, now you do it" model, in which the release of responsibility is abrupt, teacher-to-student and student-to-student interaction is minimal, and teachers do not check for student understanding (Fisher and Frey, 2008). Other ineffective lessons follow the "we do it together only" model, in which the whole class completes an assignment with little teacher modeling and few opportunities for students to practice at increasing levels of independence. In contrast, effective instruction follows a gradual release of responsibility structure that provides opportunities for teachers to check for understanding and provide immediate and specific corrective feedback to students.

There are many existing models of effective instruction. A brief discussion of several of the most respected models follows.

Hunter

Madeline Hunter (1982) popularized a model for designing and delivering lessons called "instructional theory into practice" (ITIP). ITIP encourages teachers to analyze the lesson's content, as well as specific teacher and student behaviors, to maximize learning. The instructional model, all elements of which may not be present in a single day's lesson (but may instead be represented over several days' worth of teaching and learning), has seven components:

- Objectives—define what students will be able to do at the completion of the lesson.
- Standards—describe the procedures of the lesson.
- Anticipatory set—build engagement and activate prior knowledge.
- Teaching—model and check for understanding.
- Guided practice—gradually release responsibility for learning from teacher to learner with immediate, specific, corrective feedback provided.
- Closure—synthesize new learning.
- Independent practice—begin the process of transferring learning to long-term memory.

While Hunter's model has been critiqued as a prescriptive, mechanistic, and stifling brand of teaching, it is essential as a framework to use when designing learning experiences.

Joyce, Weil, and Calhoun

Bruce Joyce, Marsha Weil, and Emily Calhoun's (2008) model of direct instruction is organized around these five phases of activity:

- Orientation—The teacher and students describe why the

lesson's objectives are relevant and upon what prior learning they build.

- Presentation—The teacher explicitly models the processes and outcomes of the new learning.

- Structured practice—The teacher and students interact as responsibility for independently learning is gradually released from the teacher to the student, with frequent opportunities for students to think, pair, and share; frequent checks for understanding; and frequent, immediate, and specific corrective feedback.

- Guided practice—Students work in various groupings (pairs, trios, small groups) with varying levels of guidance to apply the new learning, with differentiated supports based on students' levels of readiness.

- Independent practice—Students apply the new learning on tasks differentiated for their current readiness levels.

Joyce, Weil, and Calhoun's descriptions of direct instruction rest on teachers metacognitively modeling new material, students acquiring new knowledge in small steps, teachers providing a variety of ways to attack new problems, and the class staying focused on learning and avoiding distractions. Their influential textbook on instruction has influenced educators for decades.

Fisher and Frey

Douglas Fisher and Nancy Frey (2008) simplified lesson design and delivery, building on and merging research on schema (Piaget, 1952), zones of proximal development (Vygotsky, 1962,

1978), motivation (Bandura, 1965, 1977), and scaffolds (Wood, Bruner, and Ross, 1976), research that provides the foundation for all of the models described in this chapter. Fisher and Frey's model has four elements, through which responsibility is gradually released to students and in which students participate at least 50 percent of class time:

- Focus lesson—or the "I do it" model, during which teachers set the stage for the lesson and model problem solving through think-alouds.

- Guided instruction—or "we do it," during which teachers differentiate, check for understanding, and provide immediate, specific feedback.

- Collaborative learning—or "you do it together," during which teachers continue to differentiate and students negotiate learning with peers.

- Independent tasks—or "you do it alone," when students apply new learning.

Fisher and Frey's framework continues in the tradition of Hunter, with an emphasis on student involvement.

Hollingsworth and Ybarra

John Hollingsworth and Silvia Ybarra's (2009) *Explicit Direct Instruction* (EDI) model emphasizes checking for understanding throughout the lesson, in addition to specific lesson design components and the use of research-based strategies. Responsibility for learning should not be released to students, the authors note, until 80 percent of students are achieving 80 percent correct answers, with differentiated supports provided for students not yet attaining mastery. EDI lesson elements are similar to those of Hunter (1982); Joyce, Weil, and Calhoun (2008); and Fisher and Frey (2008):

- Learning objective—defining what students will be able to do by the end of the lesson.

- Activation of prior knowledge—explicitly connecting to existing schema.

- Concept development—identifying concepts underlying new learning.

- Skill development—modeling processes necessary to solve problems.

- Lesson importance—making learning relevant.

- Guided practice—solving problems *with* students in a step-by-step manner, gradually releasing responsibility, frequently checking for understanding, and providing immediate, specific, corrective feedback.

- Lesson closure—ensuring students are ready to solve problems independently.

- Independent practice—assigning practice to students that matches problems solved during the lesson.

EDI structures emphasize explicit connections among the lesson's objective, teacher modeling, guided practice, and the problems that students are expected to complete independently, thereby making their success more likely.

Goeke

Jennifer Goeke's (2008) addition to the field, *Explicit Instruction,* is a structured model in which instruction is differentiated based on students' zones of proximal development, teachers frequently check for understanding, and student engagement is emphasized. The model includes:

- Clear explanations
- Modeling the problem-solving process
- Guided practice
- Independent practice when the teacher has evidence that students can be successful
- Closure and informal or formal assessment

Every lesson may not possess all elements, and lessons may span several days, similar to Hunter. Goeke believes that explicit instruction is most appropriate when teaching well-defined skills and when students have not yet responded to other types of instruction.

THE COMPONENTS OF AN EFFECTIVE LESSON

Clarity precedes competence. Educators should reflect upon *why* the components of a Madeline Hunter lesson, and the other lesson designs described in this chapter, should be effective.

The rationale starts with a gradual release of responsibility for learning from teacher to student. To start, the teacher assumes much of the responsibility, modeling problem solving and critical thinking. Students are then brought into the problem-solving and critical-thinking process, with frequent give-and-take interactions, checks for understanding, and immediate, specific, corrective feedback. Next, students solve problems with students, receiving timely and targeted supports. Lastly, students begin reinforcing new learning, with independent practice immediately following the lesson.

However, a gradual release of responsibility is not effective unless it is focused and well defined, and unless it is relevant and connected to new learning. Therefore, we identify and communicate essential standards and "unwrap" learning targets so that instruction prepares students for mastery. And, we explicitly connect to existing schema and real-world applications so that new learning is likely to become permanent. Lastly, we check whether the release of responsibility was appropriately gradual and whether students have responded to teachers' instruction; we assess the success of the lesson and students' progress toward mastery of the lesson's objective.

There is sound theory and research behind the elements of direct instruction and the models of effective instruction described in this chapter (Hattie, 2009). There is also common-sense rationale to a structured lesson design.

KEY ELEMENTS OF EFFECTIVE INSTRUCTION

We must cease ideological objections to evidence-based practices. The elements of effective instruction described in this chapter are proven to result in increases in student learning and in all students learning at high levels. They can and must be present in any and all lessons, regardless of grade level or content area.

Before proceeding, it is critical to note that the levels of rigor, depth, and student involvement present in a well-designed lesson will not be possible if we continue to race through content. We must allow time for students to engage with content if they are to learn at the level of mastery required by the Common Core. We will not achieve this goal if we attempt to "cover" all the content in a textbook or if we attempt to "cover" all standards as if they are equally important. The organizations tasked with designing assessments for the Common Core have already identified certain standards as more essential than others; we educators must do the same. While determining essential standards and "unwrapping" standards are beyond the scope of this chapter, these practices are essential habits of teachers and schools and are prerequisites to designing and delivering effective instruction.

What follows are descriptions of seven common-sense elements of effective instruction, which have never been more important than they are in today's Common Core era:

- What are we learning? (learning targets)
- Why are we learning it? (rationale)
- I do it (teacher modeling)
- We do it together (guided instruction)
- You do it together (cooperative learning)
- You do it alone (independent practice)
- How did we do? (assessment)

What Are We Learning?

A key factor in the success of a lesson is the focus of the lesson's learning target, or objective. Lessons with objectives that are too broad or ill-defined have little chance of success. Lessons necessarily have a finite amount of time in which they are completed. When teachers attempt to help students master an inappropriately large chunk of content, frustration will ensue. When the sheer quantity of content that the class attempts to address in a lesson is too broad, teachers may move too quickly, have too little time to check for understanding, leave out explorations into greater levels of depth or complexity, and/or neglect to meet with small groups of students who require different types of support. Effective instruction and high levels of learning are impossible if a lesson's objective lacks focus. Students must have a crystal clear understanding of the focus of the lesson, and references to the lesson's objective must be made throughout the learning process; teachers should periodically refer to the objective and ask students to summarize their emerging understanding. One way of checking the focus of a lesson's objective is by determining whether a simple exit slip assigned at the conclusion of the lesson could adequately, if informally, assess student learning, and therefore the success of the lesson. Exhibit 6.1 shows the lesson design template for developing a focused lesson objective.

"Students will comprehend the story" or "Students will learn cause-and-effect" are examples of broad and unfocused objectives. "Students will utilize cause-and-effect to understand the structure of the story for the purpose of making meaning of the text" is an example of an objective that specifies how, and for what reason, a comprehension skill such as cause-and-effect will be

BOOK FIVE EXHIBIT 6.1 **A Focused Lesson Objective—What Are We Learning?**

What are the essential standards of the unit?	What is the targeted, focused objective of this lesson?	What question can assess the success of the lesson (exit slip)?

learned. This objective will also more clearly guide teachers to assess the success of the lesson.

Why Are We Learning It?

The teacher must also make clear connections to students' existing schema and to the world outside of classrooms and schools. The time it takes for teachers to plan for these connections, and the time within the lesson itself that connects to schema and the application of a lesson to students' current and future lives, are critical. Teachers can and should connect the objective to lessons from prior years, units, weeks, and days; teachers can and should also describe how an objective will help prepare the class for future learning. Teachers will wisely place some of the responsibility for making connections on students themselves; ask students to think, write, pair, and share. Learning will be inert and abstract unless teachers and students make connections. Exhibit 6.2 shows the lesson design template for connecting lessons to the real world.

BOOK FIVE EXHIBIT 6.2

Connecting to Schema and the Real World— Why Are We Learning It?

How does the lesson's objective connect to prior learning?	How does the lesson's objective connect to future learning?	How does the lesson's objective connect to real-world applications?

I Do It

Teachers must model the behaviors of an expert learner. Through enthusiastic and animated metacognitive modeling or think-alouds, teachers demonstrate for students the ways in which learning occurs. Students have the opportunity to observe a model learner—the teacher—as the teacher models critical thinking and problem solving. In the "I do it" phase, the quantity and quality of teacher talk is critical; teacher talk should be limited and should focus on demonstration and modeling. Students must clearly *see* and *hear* the thinking that is required to learn.

Students can and should be engaged during this portion of the lesson, but should typically only be involved with their voices or hands so that they are not distracted by trying to look from teacher to notebook as they attempt to keep up; students can be asked to respond chorally when questions are asking for information that they are already likely to possess. This practice will reinforce the need for students to be engaged and also connect to prior learning. If a problem type involves many steps, or if students are deemed to be restless, then the teacher should truncate the "I do it" phase, moving temporarily to the "we do it together" phase before modeling critical thinking and problem solving with a different task or problem.

Teachers can structure their think-alouds as self-dialogues that are self-questioning and self-directive. For example, a think-aloud may proceed through a series of self-questions that a teacher asks aloud (what should I do next?) and answers aloud. Alternatively, a think-aloud may proceed through a self-directive process, in which a teacher follows a set of steps or procedures. Steps are often a necessary scaffold that students need as they learn new concepts. They are not intended to mechanize learning or suggest that problem solving and critical thinking follow a rigid prescription; they can, however, provide students with a foothold when accessing new learning. Conceptual and procedural understandings are mutually reinforcing (Rittle-Johnson, Siegler, and Alibali, 2001). Steps provide procedures on which students can rely until they gain greater confidence and can include both words and pictorial supports. Teachers refer to these steps through lessons and students are encouraged to utilize them independently. Graphic organizers are research-based tools that may also be employed by the teacher and their use modeled (Marzano, Pickering, and Pollock, 2001; Hattie, 2009).

In the Common Core era, when students must be able to demonstrate their mastery of content and concepts through oral and written explanations, through graphical or pictorial supports, or through proofs of their thinking as never before, teacher modeling is more critical than ever. Teachers must explicitly model for students how to think and demonstrate mastery in this manner.

BOOK FIVE EXHIBIT 6.3 **Planning for Metacognitive Modeling—I Do It**

While solving and processing through problems before the lesson . . .		
. . . slow your thinking and record the "steps" you followed.	. . . anticipate errors and misconceptions students may have and prepare to address them.	. . . identify any visual, tactile, kinesthetic, or mnemonic supports that will aid learning.

Despite the temptation for the teacher to pause, to ask students to pair, and to address student questions, this element of effective instruction must be brief and uninterrupted. Highly interactive engagement with the lesson's objective is coming. Exhibit 6.3 shows the lesson design template for metacognitive modeling. Exhibit 6.4 shows the lesson design template for differentiating tasks.

BOOK FIVE
EXHIBIT 6.4

Differentiated Tasks—Use During I Do It, We Do It Together, You Do It Together, and You Do It Alone

Locate and list tasks that match the rigor and format of the lesson's objective for students...		
...who require prerequisite supports and more scaffolds.	...who are at the prescribed learning level, ready to engage with tasks and articulate their understanding.	...who have already begun to demonstrate mastery of the objective and are ready for enriched content.

We Do It Together

Next, teachers and students solve problems together, at first with greater levels of teacher guidance, but with less teacher voice as checks for understanding reveal increasing levels of student knowledge. Students have frequent opportunities to talk with one another. The pace and progress of the lesson are based on data: Do checks for understanding indicate that students are *responding* to the teacher's *instruction* (Fisher and Frey, 2007)? If students are not responding to instruction, the teacher takes responsibility for adjusting the type of instruction provided before asking students to work at greater levels of independence.

After teacher modeling, students should be guided to think about the content, to pair their thoughts with a partner, and to share their answers with the teacher and other students during the "we do it together" phase; this sharing provides an invaluable check for understanding to guide the pace of instruction. The tasks that teachers model during the "I do it" phase should not change dramatically throughout the lesson. Teachers follow the same procedures they modeled during the "I do it" phase, first with a tight control over the step-by-step process before releasing responsibility to students based on evidence of emerging knowledge. As evidence gathered during frequent checks for understanding reveals errors, immediate, specific, corrective feedback must follow (Duke and Pearson, 2002; Pearson and Gallagher, 1983).

Student voice, activity, and engagement must be more present in classrooms than is currently the norm. The literature (Cuban, 1993; McDonough and McDonough, 1997) on teacher talk time suggests that teachers talk for approximately 80 percent of class time and recommends that this practice be flipped, with students engaging, talking about, and practicing with new learning 80 percent of the time. Doug Fisher and Nancy Frey (2008) describe a framework within which students are talking (to each other, to the teacher, or to themselves, through oral rehearsal) during at least 50 percent of the lesson.

A simple and effective way of engaging students, checking for understanding, and monitoring the pace of the lesson is to employ think-pair-share strategies (Lyman, 1981): the teacher asks students to first think, then pair their response with their partner (with the student designated as partner A sharing first, followed by the student designated as partner B), before the teacher randomly selects a pair to share with the class. Students have numerous opportunities to think and express themselves both orally and in writing. The teacher has numerous opportunities to hear student responses, providing immediate and specific corrective feedback in a timely manner and checking for understanding to determine the appropriate pace of the lesson. Pausing a lesson and pausing teacher talk briefly is an effective way of keeping students engaged. Think-pair-share opportunities also provide students with time to synthesize new information as they talk to and listen to peers.

Monitoring students' understanding is critical throughout the lesson. It can be completed informally by randomly calling upon students to answer questions and explain their thinking during each step of the problem-solving process. It can be completed more formally midway through a lesson by using student white boards or clickers to determine our success as teachers at helping students master content, and to determine the readiness of the class and of the individual students to be released to greater levels of responsibility. Checking for understanding must be followed with immediate, specific, corrective feedback whenever errors are captured. Exhibit 6.5 shows the lesson design template for collaborative problem-solving, monitoring of student understanding, and feedback.

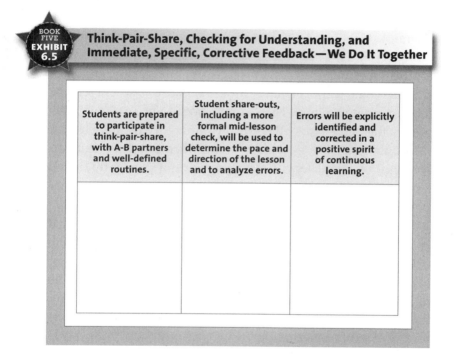

BOOK FIVE EXHIBIT 6.5

Think-Pair-Share, Checking for Understanding, and Immediate, Specific, Corrective Feedback—We Do It Together

Students are prepared to participate in think-pair-share, with A-B partners and well-defined routines.	Student share-outs, including a more formal mid-lesson check, will be used to determine the pace and direction of the lesson and to analyze errors.	Errors will be explicitly identified and corrected in a positive spirit of continuous learning.

You Do It Together

Students should be provided with structured cooperative learning opportunities. Reciprocal teaching (Palincsar & Brown, 1984a, 1984b) and literature circles (Daniels, 2002) represent research-based and proven sets of procedures for organizing student interactions, and students should have time to work in groups on common problems in any lesson. This interaction can begin with a few simple tasks; for example, groups of four students can individually complete a math problem before sharing results with each other. If all students are in agreement, one student explains the method of solving the problem, explaining the how and the why to other group members. If there are different answers, students representing the different solutions take turns presenting their solutions and errors are identified and analyzed. In reading comprehension, groups of students could identify and contribute a cause or effect in relation to a key event in a story. These comprehension groups could then present their analysis to other small groups or to the entire class.

Many teachers express frustration when tasks that students are asked to complete with their peers or independently lead to quizzical looks or incomplete work. This may occur because tasks or strategies that teachers utilize during the "I do it" and "we do it together" phases do not match textbook-based worksheets that are assigned later in the lesson. This disconnect leads to confusion (students raising their hands, completing the task incorrectly, or disengaging from the assignment). Thus, while students should ultimately be able to transfer their learning to unique contexts, the continuity of a task from the beginning to the end of the lesson is a critical consideration.

"You do it together" can be differentiated; different groups of students can be given distinct tasks that represent students' zones of proximal development. Or, a teacher may determine that some students are not yet ready to be released to this level of responsibility. They may benefit from more guided practice, or more "we do it together." Therefore, the teacher can serve as the leader of a group of students who have these needs.

The point of "you do it together" is to provide students with the responsibility to negotiate their learning with other students. Students collaborate, compromise, explain their thinking, and analyze errors. And importantly, they are speaking to and hearing from classmates, not from the teacher. "You do it together" places greater responsibility on students, but these interactions will not be productive without clear expectations that are modeled and practiced. Teachers should demonstrate the behaviors of an effective team by playing the role of a student in a group. They should fishbowl the behaviors of an effective group by asking students to positively critique one student group that "performs" for the rest

BOOK FIVE EXHIBIT 6.6 Routines and Immediate Support—You Do It Together

How has the class been prepared to work together in small groups with a high degree of autonomy?	How do students interact with other students and share their thinking with the class?	How do you identify students requiring more "we do it together" support? How is this support provided?

of the class. Students of all ages can learn with and from their classmates when we set high and clear expectations. The Common Core State Standards include a special emphasis on listening and speaking because of their intrinsic value as both modes of communication and prerequisites of reading and writing. Therefore, the time spent in class in the "you do it together" phase is valuable and necessary. Exhibit 6.6 shows the lesson design template for supporting collaborative student learning.

You Do It Alone

Based on an evaluation of student success during the "you do it together" phase and an understanding of student needs, teachers should assign independent practice. Homework has been a topic of some controversy, but this need not be the case. Teachers must have evidence and confidence that "you do it alone" assignments, including homework, can be completed independently by students. Students will likely work on independent practice tasks both in and out of class. These tasks should serve to reinforce tasks completed during the school day, cementing learning and assisting in the transfer from short-term to long-term memory (Anderson, 2000). If evidence exists that students are not ready to successfully complete the planned homework independently—or, said another way, if there is a lack of evidence that students can successfully and independently engage with tasks related to the lesson—an alternative "you do it alone" task should be assigned, or no task should be assigned.

Our knowledge of zones of proximal development and our knowledge of our students both suggest that we should not be assigning the same "you do it alone" tasks to all students. We ac-

knowledge that we commonly have students in classes scoring between the 5th and 95th percentile on norm-referenced tests. We
recognize that we should be differentiating instruction based on,
among other factors, student readiness. It follows that we must
assign different types of tasks as homework. These "you do it
alone" tasks should match the rigor and format of the types of
tasks that students have completed throughout the lesson. Students may complete different problems or questions within a single assignment. They may be asked to perform different tasks with
the same content. A single homework assignment for all is bound
to be a mismatch for two-thirds of students, those requiring more
scaffolded support and those ready to extend their learning. We
must differentiate "you do it alone" tasks to match our differentiated instruction.

How Did We Do?

The success of a lesson can only be determined by the extent to
which students have learned the topics, concepts, or skills that the
teacher has taught. In other words, was the objective ("what are
we learning?") met? A simple exit slip or ticket out the door, completed on a self-adhesive note, notecard, or piece of scrap paper,
can answer many important questions, including the following:

- How effective was the instruction in the lesson?
- Does the class need to revisit these topics, concepts, and
  skills during subsequent lessons?
- What types of errors do students seem to be making?
- Assuming the instruction was effective for most, which
  students are not yet responding to instruction?

As is the case with all assessments, students should be involved. One idea is to ask students to self-assess (either before the "how did we do?" question is answered, or after, or both) their progress toward meeting the objective on a one-to-five scale, including a simple strategy they will employ to continue their learning. Exhibit 6.7 shows the lesson design template for using exit slips.

Effective instruction, as measured by student learning, will be more likely to occur when teachers plan and implement a lesson that includes the elements described in this chapter. A sample lesson that follows the steps of effective instruction for a seventh-grade math class is included in Exhibit 6.8.

BOOK FIVE
EXHIBIT
6.7

Administering and Analyzing Exit Slips—How Did We Do?

What method of checking for the efficacy of the lesson do you employ (exit slip, ticket-out-the-door, clickers)?	What tasks, if any, are assigned to students if they are not ready to complete the planned homework (the "you do it alone" assignment)?	How is the evidence gathered during the "how did we do?" checks used to inform future instruction?

BOOK FIVE EXHIBIT 6.8

Example of Direct Instruction— Seventh-Grade Math Lesson

A Focused Lesson Objective—What Are We Learning?

What are the essential standards of the unit?	What is the targeted, focused objective of this lesson?	What question can assess the success of the lesson (exit slip)?
• Create scenarios that include positive numbers and their additive inverses (7NS1). • Add and subtract integers using multiple strategies (7NS1). • Create real-world scenarios involving the addition and subtraction of integers and negative rational numbers (7NS3). • Know and apply the rules for multiplying and dividing signed rational numbers (7NS2).	I can add and subtract integers.	What is -8 + -5? Show your work using the "steps." Prove your answer with a number line.

Connecting to Schema and the Real World— Why Are We Learning It?

How does the lesson's objective connect to prior learning?	How does the lesson's objective connect to future learning?	How does the lesson's objective connect to real-world applications?
• Adding and subtracting integers is based on the same rules as adding and subtracting whole numbers. • A number line would demonstrate that adding and subtracting integers will simply require that we move to the left of zero.	Adding and subtracting integers will help us: • Add and subtract other signed rational numbers, like decimals and fractions. • Understand the positions of coordinates in the Cartesian plane. • Solve equations.	• Integers are used in computer programming—a computer's screen can be thought of as a Cartesian plane. • Mastering operations with integers makes solving equations a snap.

BOOK FIVE
EXHIBIT 6.8

Example of Direct Instruction—
Seventh-Grade Math Lesson (Continued)

Planning for Metacognitive Modeling—I Do It

While solving and processing through problems before the lesson . . .

. . . slow your thinking and record the "steps" you followed.	. . . anticipate errors and misconceptions students may have and prepare to address them.	. . . identify any visual, tactile, kinesthetic, or mnemonic supports that will aid learning.
Rules for adding and subtracting integers: $\left.\begin{matrix} +\ + \\ -\ - \end{matrix}\right\}$ + add $\left.\begin{matrix} +\ - \\ -\ + \end{matrix}\right\}$ − subtract * The sign of the number with the greater absolute value will be the sign of the answer. **Step 1:** Circle the two signs in the middle of the expression. **Step 2:** If the circled signs are the same, change them to an addition sign. If the circled signs are different, change them to a subtraction sign. −8 + ⁺3 −8 ⊕ ³3 −8 + 3 ****************************** −5 − ⁺2 −5 ⊖ ³2 −5 − 2	• Students may incorrectly interpret "addition" for "subtraction," and vice versa. • Use "moving to the left or right" on a number line. • Students may assign the wrong sign to the answer. • Reinforce the concept of absolute value.	• Students can use their arms to "point" in the direction that the operation sign and number sign are directing them to move "on the number line." • Students can draw number lines in their notebooks as a guide. • Students can use red cubes to represent negative numbers and blue cubes to represent positive numbers— equal numbers of cubes "cancel each other out."

Example of Direct Instruction—
Seventh-Grade Math Lesson *(Continued)*

Planning for Metacognitive Modeling—I Do It		
While solving and processing through problems before the lesson . . .		
. . . slow your thinking and record the "steps" you followed.	. . . anticipate errors and misconceptions students may have and prepare to address them.	. . . identify any visual, tactile, kinesthetic, or mnemonic supports that will aid learning.
*********************** −6 + ⁻4 −6 ⊕ ⁻4 −6 − 4 *********************** −7 + ⁻6 −7 ⊖ ⁻6 −7 + 6 **Step 3**: Look at the remaining signs. If they are both the same, add the absolute values of the two numbers. If the two signs are different, subtract the two absolute values of the numbers. **Step 4**: The number with the greatest absolute value will have its sign carried into the answer. −8 + 3 (− and + ; *subtract*) −5 *********************** −5 − 2 (− and − ; *add*) −7 *********************** −6 − 4 (− and − ; *add*) −10 *********************** −7 + 6 (− and + ; *subtract*) −1		

Example of Direct Instruction—
Seventh-Grade Math Lesson *(Continued)*

Differentiated Tasks—Use During I Do It, We Do It Together, You Do It Together, and You Do It Alone

Locate and list tasks that match the rigor and format of the lesson's objective for students...

...who require prerequisite supports and more scaffolds.	...who are at the prescribed learning level, ready to engage with tasks and articulate their understanding.	...who have already begun to demonstrate mastery of the objective and are ready for enriched content.
$^-1 + 2$ $^-3 + 4$ $7 + {^-6}$	$-45 + {^-31}$ Jorge had $3,400 in his bank account. He spent $1,600 on a used car. How much money does he have left in his account? Express each of the money amounts using integer signs. Prove your answer by describing the rules, providing a proof, or using a picture, drawing, model, or diagram.	Evaluate the following expression. Prove your answer by describing the rules or providing a proof. $^-15 + 23 - {^-8} + 9$ Then, describe a real-life situation that the expression could describe.

BOOK FIVE EXHIBIT 6.8

Example of Direct Instruction— Seventh-Grade Math Lesson *(Continued)*

Think-Pair-Share, Checking for Understanding, and Immediate, Specific, Corrective Feedback—We Do It Together

Students are prepared to participate in think-pair-share, with A-B partners and well-defined routines.	Student share-outs, including a more formal mid-lesson check, will be used to determine the pace and direction of the lesson and to analyze errors.	Errors will be explicitly identified and corrected in a positive spirit of continuous learning.
• Students are seated heterogeneously at tables of four, next to and across from a student close to their zone of proximal development, and will "pair" with their A-B partner both across and beside. • During "you do it together," students may work in more homogenous groups on differentiated tasks. • Students will always be randomly selected to respond after 1) a question has been asked, 2) students have had a brief opportunity to think and then 3) share with an A-B partner.	• The following problem will be used as a mid-lesson check for understanding to take the "pulse" of the lesson: Jose began the game with 20 points, but lost 40 points. How many points does he have? Use a number line to support your answer. • Students will answer the question on their white boards without assistance. If fewer than approximately 80 percent of students answer correctly and completely, we will cycle back to "we do it together." Students requiring more support will meet with the teacher during "you do it together."	• Errors made will be known as "opportunities for learning." • The teacher will immediately, clearly, and specifically identify and correct the error, explaining why the error may have been made (referencing the "steps for adding and subtracting integers" poster and using the number line), before moving on to the next step of the problem.

BOOK FIVE
EXHIBIT 6.8

Example of Direct Instruction— Seventh-Grade Math Lesson *(Continued)*

Routines and Immediate Support—You Do It Together

How has the class been prepared to work together in small groups with a high degree of autonomy?	How do students interact with other students and share their thinking with the class?	How do you identify students requiring more "we do it together" support? How is this support provided?
• The teacher will post the expectations and roles of students when working with peers. • One student will serve as team captain, responsible for gathering any necessary materials and recording questions that the group cannot answer. • The team captain role will rotate weekly. • Teams will not interrupt the teacher while the teacher is working with a small group, saving questions until the end of the lesson. • Periodically (monthly unless needed more frequently), the teacher will reteach and remodel the behaviors of an effective group by: • Playing the role of a student in a group in front of the class. • Fishbowling the behaviors of an effective group for the rest of the class. • Class will conclude by positively reinforcing effective teams and constructively critiquing less-than-desired actions.	• Each team will have one white board and one white board marker. • When a question arises, the team captain will ask for a volunteer to demonstrate the solution on the white board. • When teams complete all tasks, students will take turns with the white board explaining their solutions. • Other extension tasks are available for students when they complete "you do it together" tasks early. • Time permitting, the teacher will randomly select students to explain solutions to "you do it together" tasks to the entire class.	• The mid-unit checks for understanding—(Jose began the game with 20 points, but lost 40 points. How many points does he have? Use a number line to support your answer.)—will be used to identify students who may not be ready to work in groups. • Students who do not answer this question completely and correctly will work in a small group with the teacher to complete tasks with guidance. • If necessary, prerequisite skills will be reviewed. • Personal number lines and colored cubes will be used to scaffold learning. • If no students require more guided support, the teacher can meet with on-level and above-level students to work with the enriched content described above.

BOOK FIVE
EXHIBIT 6.8

Example of Direct Instruction—
Seventh-Grade Math Lesson *(Continued)*

Administering and Analyzing Exit Slips—How Did We Do?

What method of checking for the efficacy of the lesson do you employ (exit slip, ticket-out-the-door, clickers)?	What tasks, if any, are assigned to students if they are not ready to complete the planned homework (the "you do it alone" assignment)?	How is the evidence gathered during the "how did we do?" checks used to inform future instruction?
• The success of the class at meeting the lesson's objective (and the success of the lesson itself) will be assessed with the following prompt: What is -8 + -5? Show your work using the "steps." Prove your answer with a number line. • Students will record their answers on pieces of scrap paper and hand them in as they quietly line up at the door prior to dismissal from class.	If the entire class, or individual students, are deemed to be unable to complete planned homework tasks independently, these students will practice the eight-question "Review of 6th-Grade Math" sheets that the middle school math team created. The Common Core State Standards were written with the "coherence" of standards in mind. It is possible that 6th-grade content will represent prerequisite skills with which 7th-grade students are experiencing difficulty.	• Exit slips will be quickly analyzed to determine: • Which students appear to have met the lesson's objective. • Whether approximately 80 percent of the class met the objective, so that the next day's lesson—applications of adding and subtracting integers—can be completed, or if another day of this lesson's objective is necessary.

TEACHING BEHAVIOR

Behavior and academics are inextricably linked. This is particularly true for students at risk (Buffum, Mattos, and Weber, 2009, 2010, 2012; Hierck, Coleman, and Weber, 2011; Weber, 2013). When students are not responding to core instruction in essential academic content, the causes of these difficulties may be deficits in basic academic needs—students may have deficits in reading, writing, number sense, or English language that are compromising their ability to access content or demonstrate mastery. Alternatively, students who are not responding to core instruction in essential academic content may simply need more time and/or differentiated supports.

Another possibility that we must consider is that students' misbehavior, in the domain of either social or academic behaviors (e.g., self-regulatory strategies or executive functioning skills), is inhibiting their success in mastering grade-level or content essentials. It is rare to find a student whose academic difficulties have not led to behavioral challenges; it is equally rare to find a student whose inappropriate behaviors do not significantly impede learning. We must accept responsibility for teaching students the social and academic behaviors that we want to see. While a full exploration of social and academic behaviors is well beyond the scope of this chapter, it is entirely appropriate to note that behaviors must be taught in the same manner as academics. The principles of effective academic instruction described here also apply to teaching students to behave in a manner that will keep them on track to graduate from high school ready for college or a skilled career.

SUMMARY

For all students to learn at the levels of depth and complexity required by the Common Core, well-designed and well-delivered instruction is paramount. Effective instruction makes learning targets clear to students and to the teacher, provides a rationale for the learning, and connects new knowledge to existing knowledge. It allows students to observe a model learner (the teacher) in action, and it provides the teacher with multiple opportunities to check for understanding; provide immediate, specific, corrective feedback; evaluate current levels of student proficiency; and differentiate instruction. It allows students to work with peers and engage with new content under the watchful eye of their teacher. It includes appropriate, targeted independent practice, and end-of-lesson assessments to guide future instruction. Effective instruction may span days; it may be organized around small groups of students within the classroom; it may occur in a variety of sequences; but effective instruction always possesses the attributes described in this chapter.

Highly effective Tier 1 instruction is a fundamental component of Response to Intervention (RTI) (Buffum, Mattos, & Weber, 2009). To ensure that a student's challenges are not the result of inadequately planned and insufficiently differentiated teaching, an increased focus on pedagogy must accompany our implementation of the Common Core. Remember: the most critical tier of RTI is Tier 1, and the best intervention is prevention.

References

Ainsworth, L. (2003). *"Unwrapping" the standards: A simple process to make standards manageable.* Englewood, CO: Lead + Learn Press.

Ainsworth, L. (2013). *Prioritizing the Common Core: Identifying the specific standards that matter most.* Englewood, CO: Lead + Learn Press.

Anderson, J. R. (2000). *Learning and memory: An integrated approach.* New York, NY: John Wiley & Sons.

Bandura, A. (1965). Influence of models' reinforcement contingencies on the acquisition of imitative responses. *Journal of Personality and Social Psychology, 1,* 589–595.

Bandura, A. (1977). *Social learning theory.* Englewood Cliffs, NJ: Prentice Hall.

Black, P., & Wiliam, D. (1998). Inside the black box: Raising standards through classroom assessment. *Phi Delta Kappan, 80*(2), 139–148.

Buffum, A., Mattos, M., & Weber, C. (2009). *Pyramid response to intervention: RTI, professional learning communities, and how to respond when kids don't learn.* Bloomington, IN: Solution Tree.

Buffum, A., Mattos, M., & Weber, C. (2010). The why behind RTI. *Educational Leadership, 68*(2), 10–16.

Buffum, A., Mattos, M., & Weber, C. (2012). *Simplifying response to intervention: Four essential guiding principles.* Bloomington, IN: Solution Tree.

City, E. A., Elmore, R. F., Fiarman, S. E., & Teitel, L. (2009). *Instructional rounds in education: A network approach to improving teaching and learning.* Cambridge, MA: Harvard Education Press.

Cuban, L. (1993). *How teachers teach: Constancy and change in American classrooms, 1890-1990.* New York: Teachers College Press.

Daniels, H. (2002). *Literature circles: Voice and choice in book clubs and reading groups.* Portland, ME: Stenhouse.

Doyle, W. (1983). Academic work. *Review of Educational Research, 53*(2), 159–199.

Duke, N. K., & Pearson, P. D. (2002). Effective practices for developing reading comprehension. In A. E. Farstup & S. J. Samuels (Eds.), *What research has to say about reading instruction* (pp. 205–242). Newark, DE: International Reading Association.

Elmore, R. (2010). Leading the instructional core: A conversation with Richard Elmore. *In Conversation, 11*(3).

Fisher, D., & Frey, N. (2007). *Checking for understanding: Formative assessment techniques for your classroom.* Alexandria, VA: Association for Supervision and Curriculum Development.

Fisher, D., & Frey, N. (2008). *Better learning through structured teaching: A framework for the gradual release of responsibility.* Alexandria, VA: Association for Supervision and Curriculum Development.

Goeke, J. L. (2008). *Explicit instruction: A framework for meaningful direct teaching.* Upper Saddle River, NJ: Pearson.

Hattie, J. (2009). *Visible learning: A synthesis of over 800 meta-analyses relating to student achievement.* New York, NY: Routledge.

Hierck, T., Coleman, C., & Weber, C. (2011). *Pyramid of behavior interventions: 7 keys to a positive learning environment.* Bloomington, IN: Solution Tree.

Hollingsworth, J., & Ybarra, S. (2009). *Explicit direct instruction (EDI): The power of the well-crafted, well-taught lesson.* Thousand Oaks, CA: Corwin.

Hunter, M. (1982). *Mastery teaching.* El Segundo, CA: TIP Publications.

Joyce, B., Weil, M., & Calhoun, E. (2008). *Models of teaching* (8th ed.). Boston: Allyn & Bacon.

Leithwood K., Anderson S., Mascall, B., & Strauss, T. (2010). School leaders' influences on student learning: The four paths. In T. Bush, L. Bell, & D. Middlewood (Eds.), *The principles of educational leadership and management.* London: Sage.

Lyman, F. (1981). The responsive classroom discussion: The inclusion of all students. In A. Anderson (Ed.), *Mainstreaming Digest* (pp. 109–113). College Park, MD: University of Maryland Press.

Marzano, R. J. (2003). *What works in schools: Translating research into action.* Alexandria, VA: Association for Supervision and Curriculum Development.

Marzano, R. J., Pickering, D. J., & Pollock, J. E. (2001). *Classroom instruction that works: Research-based strategies for increasing student achievement.* Alexandria, VA: Association for Supervision and Curriculum Development.

McDonough, J., & McDonough, S. (1997). *Research methods for English language teachers.* London: Arnold.

Newmann, F. M., & Wehlage, G. G. (1993). Five standards of authentic instruction. *Educational Leadership, 50*(7), 8–12.

Palinscar, A. S., & Brown, A. L. (1984a). Interactive teaching to promote independent learning from text. *The Reading Teacher, 39,* 771–777.

Palinscar, A., & Brown, A. (1984b). Reciprocal teaching of comprehension-fostering and comprehension-monitoring activities. *Cognition and Instruction, 1*(2), 117–175.

Pearson, P. D., & Gallagher, M. C. (1983). The instruction of reading comprehension. *Contemporary Educational Psychology, 8,* 317–344.

Piaget, J. (1952). *The origins of intelligence in children.* New York, NY: Norton.

Reeves, D. B. (2006). *The learning leader: How to focus school improvement for better results.* Alexandria, VA: Association for Supervision and Curriculum Development.

Rittle-Johnson, B., Siegler, R. S., & Alibali, M. W. (2001). Developing conceptual understanding and procedural skill in mathematics: An iterative process. *Journal of Educational Psychology, 93*(2), 346–362.

Tomlinson, C. A. (2001). *How to differentiate instruction in mixed-ability classrooms* (2nd ed.). Alexandria, VA: Association for Supervision and Curriculum Development.

Vygotsky, L. S. (1962). *Thought and language.* Cambridge, MA: MIT Press.

Vygotsky, L. S. (1978). *Mind in society.* Cambridge, MA: Harvard University Press.

Weber, C. (2013). *RTI and the early grades: Intervention strategies for mathematics, literacy, behavior, and fine-motor challenges.* Bloomington, IN: Solution Tree.

Wood, D., Bruner, J. S., & Ross, G. (1976). The role of tutoring and problem solving. *Journal of Child Psychology and Psychiatry, 17,* 89–100.

CHAPTER SEVEN

Students with Disabilities: Moving Your Numbers

Deborah M. Telfer and Brian McNulty

Most educators agree that the new Common Core State Standards are better than previous standards in a number of ways, including clarity, sequencing, and higher expectations for students and teachers. At the same time, the higher performance levels expected of all students will prove challenging, especially for students who are not meeting the current standards and expectations. While this is true of many subgroups, students identified as having a disability that could affect their learning and other marginalized groups of learners that have similar challenges are most at risk of not meeting the new standards and expectations.

In an effort to help identify what improves the performance of students with disabilities, a number of educators came together to identify and examine school districts with continuously improving student achievement levels. The Moving Your Numbers project (www.movingyournumbers.org), funded by the National Center on Educational Outcomes and coordinated through the University of Dayton School of Education and Health Sciences Grant Center, was initiated in 2011 to identify a range of demographically different school districts from across the country that were using assessment and accountability as a way to improve performance for all students in their districts. Exhibit 7.1 lists the districts involved.

BOOK FIVE EXHIBIT 7.1   **Districts Featured in Moving Your Numbers**

Bartholomew Consolidated School Corporation, Columbus, Indiana

Bloom Vernon Local Schools, South Webster, Ohio

Brevard Public Schools, Viera, Florida

Gwinnett County Public Schools, Suwanee, Georgia

Lake Villa School District 41, Lake Villa, Illinois

Somersworth/Rollinsford School System [School Administrative Unit (SAU) 56], Somersworth, New Hampshire

Stoughton Area School District, Stoughton, Wisconsin

Tigard-Tualatin School District, Tigard, Oregon

Val Verde Unified School District, Perris, California

Wooster City School District, Wooster, Ohio

While each of these districts is unique in its needs and strategies, what became clear was that each of them uses a number of specific, essential practices. These six practices, when used in an aligned and coherent way, resulted in higher achievement for all students (McNulty and Besser, 2011):

• Use data well and in an ongoing way.

- Focus your goals.
- Select and implement shared instructional practices.
- Implement deeply.
- Monitor, provide feedback, and provide support.
- Inquire and learn (at the district, school, and teacher team levels).

The project also identified a number of underlying assumptions to guide their work (Telfer, 2011). The assumptions are summarized below.

- Successful outcomes (including college and career readiness) for students receiving special education services require their inclusion in standards-based reform efforts and their participation in statewide assessment and accountability systems.
- Improving the educational outcomes of students receiving special education services, as for any other group, requires a sustained focus on teaching and learning, aligned actions across the district, and continuous monitoring of the degree of implementation of those actions to assess their impact on student learning.
- Students receiving special education services are as different from each other as the members of any other group; assuming predetermined levels of achievement based on disability status limits these students' opportunity to learn and diminishes the collective responsibility of adults to provide high-quality instruction aligned with grade-level content to these students.

• Consistent, high-quality implementation of effective practices is a challenge for many districts.

Guided by the above practices and assumptions, the group began to identify school districts that were making consistent progress with students with disabilities. What follows is a discussion of the six essential practices, accompanied by specific examples from the featured districts (hereafter referred to as project districts). These practices are taken from McNulty and Besser (2011).

USE DATA WELL
AND IN AN ONGOING WAY

The first essential practice is "use data well," but in addition to being used well, data are used continuously by these districts in their application of all of the essential practices. Data are used in an ongoing way to do the following:

• Establish goals (for the district, buildings and classrooms).

• Guide discussions about instructional practices.

• Monitor the implementation and effectiveness of teacher, building, and district leadership teams.

• Monitor the implementation and evaluate the impact of the improvement strategies.

• Provide feedback to staff on the strategies and teams and their impact.

• Assess the effectiveness of the professional development supports that are provided.

Data are used to identify district-wide and building-wide needs and to measure the degree of implementation and ongoing progress in addressing those needs (see Exhibit 7.2). What you see in these districts is that data are used at every level of the system to provide feedback on the effectiveness of their efforts. They view the collection of data as "feedback to the system." They use their data pragmatically. If they are making progress, they keep doing what they're doing. If they are not making progress, they try something different and then evaluate that. Within each of the

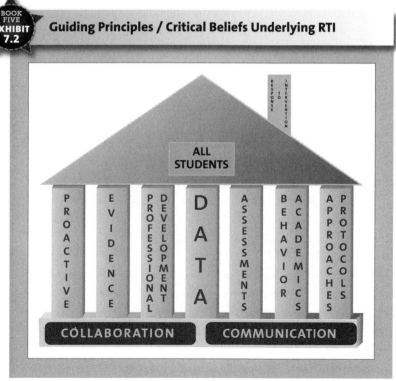

BOOK FIVE
EXHIBIT 7.2

Guiding Principles / Critical Beliefs Underlying RTI

Source: SAU 56, Somersworth, NH.

essential practices you will see the use of data. In many of these districts, they use monitoring data to assess how well they are implementing the improvement strategies they have chosen. These data then inform school and district leadership teams as to their progress and next steps. A variety of frameworks (e.g., Response to Intervention [RTI], Ohio Improvement Process) were used by Moving Your Numbers districts. In every case, data use was a critical element of the district's work to get focused and make improvements.

In Somersworth, New Hampshire, SAU 56 Superintendent Jeni Mosca believes that more strategic data use was instrumental in helping the school administrative unit (SAU) move beyond preference and opinion to identify the real issues that needed to be addressed. "Data allowed us to look at ourselves in the mirror in an honest way. We have tons of data and we're moving away from collecting all kinds of data to becoming much more intentional and collecting what we need to make better decisions about instruction," she said. Effective data use is characterized as a primary pillar upon which the SAU's instructional and improvement framework is built.

SAU 56, like the other districts profiled by the project, acknowledged the vast amount of data and information bombarding districts today. The idea of becoming much more strategic in using the right data for ongoing instructional improvement and decision making is a theme across all the featured districts, and is reflected in the sentiments and actions of the Bloom Vernon Local School District and the Lake Villa School District 41 leadership. "We're careful not to give too much data; the data we want teachers to use must be relevant," said Alex Barbour, Assistant Superintendent at Lake Villa School District 41. "Weighing the pig won't make it fatter," remarked Scott Holstein, Principal of Bloom Vernon's South Webster Elementary School. "We look at data to pinpoint areas of need, develop goals, and track progress, rather than using data for data's sake," added Holstein.

In the Tigard-Tualatin School District, the ninth largest district in Oregon, a district-wide culture of continuous improvement has evolved around the consistent and prescriptive use of data, not only to identify critical needs, but also to gauge progress and make decisions about what is and is not working well instructionally. "Seeing the data reinforces staff belief in the system," said Laura Kintz, Principal of Alberta Rider Elementary School. District protocols are established and used by teams across the district to improve fidelity of implementation. "We don't leave a child's academic or social development to chance based on whose classroom or which school they happen to attend," explained Dan Goldman, Director of Curriculum and Instruction. A Response to Intervention framework is used by both Tigard-Tualatin and SAU 56, with data use aligned to the framework and systematized at all levels of the organizations. Both districts have been supported in the development of their instructional models by state initiatives focused on RTI and have, in turn, influenced their states' refinement and use of such models with other districts.

The ongoing use of assessment data to increase academic achievement for all groups of students was key to Gwinnett County Public Schools' receipt of the 2010 Broad Prize for urban education. Dr. Jeff Barker, Executive Director of Accountability and Assessment, explains: "We can't wait until test data are released to identify and prioritize our needs and plan for how to respond instructionally." With more than 130 school buildings in the district, Gwinnett has an extensive assessment program and has reconceptualized the way staff think about assessment, moving away from the idea of testing as an event, to thinking about assessment as a continuous part of the instructional process. This shift in thinking is reflected in the placement of the office of assessment and accountability as part of the division of teaching and learning support.

Similarly, in the Stoughton Area School District and the Val Verde Unified School District the placement of staff assigned to support higher achievement for students receiving special education services was intentionally restructured to be subsumed within the larger departments/divisions responsible for teaching and learning across the districts. In Stoughton, a data utilization specialist was designated to facilitate and monitor effective use of common classroom formative assessment, as well as state and district assessment, by all personnel, and to respond to the district's stated strategy of "driving instructional improvement and facilitating communication with district stakeholders by supporting and expecting staff to access and utilize student data effectively."

In the Val Verde Unified School District, staff recognized that state assessment data, while important in identifying trends and critical needs, were insufficient for making ongoing decisions about instructional design and delivery. "Our focus on looking at data is to develop our plan for getting to 100 percent proficiency," said Deborah Bryant, Director of Assessment and Accountability. Val Verde, like other larger districts featured (e.g., Gwinnett County Public Schools, Brevard Public Schools), has Web-based district data systems in place to support the ongoing use of a variety of aligned and connected data by teachers, administrators, and related service personnel. Such systems align data from a variety of assessments with standards-based curricular materials and decision-making protocols.

These systems also facilitate the use of critical data by teams at the district, school, and teacher levels and are increasingly being used to structure the sharing of information among teams. In Wooster, Ohio, the Wooster City School District used the state's improvement process (called the Ohio Improvement Process) and associated major tools (e.g., the Ohio Decision Framework) to home in on the most important issues. "Using the [Ohio] Decision Framework helped us look at data in a very different way, versus just having a theory or an opinion of what was happening with students," explained Rich Leone, Wooster's Director of Secondary Education. "If I heard it once, I heard it many times—it was powerful for teams to look at district-wide data, rather than having buildings look only at their own building-level data. That district-wide view was essential in moving toward collective ownership for the work of the district," added Leone. And, it was essential in facilitating shared responsibility for the success of all students. In Bloom Vernon Local, a small Appalachian district in southern Ohio, South Webster Junior/Senior High Principal Bob Johnson explained: "We began to focus on the data ... we had always paid attention to student learning, but we started to focus on the kids who weren't achieving." Bloom Vernon Local is characterized by regional service providers in southern Ohio as one of the districts that pioneered the use of data to look at the learning needs of individual children.

Engaging all personnel in using data to make decisions about how to more effectively and collectively support higher levels of learning for all students is paying off. "Accessibility of data has changed the conversation across the district," said Cynthia Van Meter, Associate Superintendent of Curriculum and Instruction for Brevard Public Schools. The power of effective data use in changing the way in which adults work together is also reflected in one of the district's operational beliefs: "Revere data that provide feedback to students, inform programmatic and instructional decisions, and support focused intervention efforts."

In all districts featured—from the largest to the smallest—expectations and requirements for effective data use were made clear by district leadership. "Data drive the decision-making process," said Dr. John Van Pelt, Superintendent of Lake Villa School District 41 until the 2013–2014 school year. Regardless of each district's belief about the value of federal or state-imposed accountability systems, all districts agree that use of data is essential. In the Bartholomew Consolidated School Corporation, a variety of formative and summative data and artifacts are reviewed regularly to ensure that students are on track, and to support higher levels of learning for all students. Exhibit 7.3, from Bartholomew Consolidated School Corporation, shows data on specific performance gains for students with disabilities across a four-year period. While this district has clearly made significant gains, they still recognize the need to continue to collect data on both their implementation strategies and the performance outcomes for their students to assess their progress.

Bartholomew Consolidated's Director of Secondary Education Bill Jensen and Director of Special Education Dr. George Van Horn agree that effective data use is a key strategy for continuous improvement. Jensen said, and Van Horn agreed, "We're committed to making sure the curriculum and instruction is for all students; we want growth for everyone." Clearly, districts that are

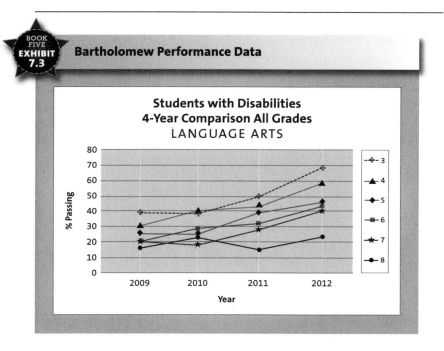

making continuous progress for all students understand that collaboration, informed by data, is essential to their progress. They also understand that the purpose of data collection is to make better decisions and to take action. These districts don't just collect data, they act on the data.

FOCUS YOUR GOALS

Stated simply, most school and district improvement plans have too many goals and strategies (Reeves, 2010.) Recently, a number of educational researchers have all come to the same conclusion: districts and schools that make progress *focus* (Fullan, 2009; Levin, 2009; Reeves, 2011; McNulty and Besser, 2011; Schmoker, 2011).

Reeves (2009) says that "complex organizations that create meaningful change in a short period of time are not weighed down by voluminous strategic plans; they have absolute clarity about a very few things that must be done immediately" (p. 243). He also argues that, based on a double-blind review of more than 2,000 schools, schools with higher levels of focus not only have higher levels of student achievement, but are also better able to implement other essential leadership and teaching strategies. He makes a convincing claim that "focus is the first obligation of leaders" (Reeves, 2011, p. 75). The districts cited in the following examples exemplify this kind of focus by limiting the number of goals and strategies that they undertake. In doing so, they push their organizations to go deeper into their learning about their implementation.

"Common," "shared," "collective," and "universal" are among the words used by featured districts to describe their approach to improving outcomes for all students. Each district identified an organizing framework that was used to foster collective action on the part of adults across the system and to make decisions about what should and shouldn't be an area of focus for the district.

Every district identified the need to focus on fewer, more relevant pieces of work, and to align that core work in ways that would improve coherence and consistency in the instruction provided to all students. As exemplified by Superintendent Van Pelt, "Being focused in Lake Villa means using a systemic approach that is grounded in a framework or guiding set of procedures that guides the district." In the Bartholomew Consolidated School Corporation, personnel learned early that a framework was needed to align and improve coherence, while bringing staff together around shared priorities. "We tried to squeeze everything into our school improvement plans before; we learned the importance of having a framework," said Darin Sprong, Principal of Richards Elementary School.

Mobilizing staff through closely held shared beliefs is expressed in Bloom Vernon Superintendent Rick Carrington's reference to the power of unification around purpose. Carrington explains: "I believe in the power of unification around purpose and ours is to help all kids learn at high levels. Our greatest challenge involves eliminating the mindset that because we're poor and rural, kids can't achieve."

In the Stoughton Area School District, gaining focus around core work was facilitated by the development of a common philosophy grounded in a social justice framework. "We went from having no common philosophy to creating a unified message and embedding what was a separate office for special education within the department of teaching and learning," said Dr. Kurt Schneider, former Director of Student Services. Like Stoughton, Val Verde Unified moved special education functions under the larger Department of Educational Services to send the clear message that the district's core instructional program was for every student in the district. Districts like Stoughton and Val Verde that have made progress for students with disabilities have taken steps to create a unified system of education where adults in the system share in the collective responsibility for the success of every student. Rather than using a more traditional departmental or programmatic approach based on label or funding source, such districts have focused on creating a system of supports for meeting the needs of all students.

Moving from multiple goals and initiatives to three goals that are used to structure the work across the district is what Dr. Michael Tefs, Superintendent/CEO of the Wooster City School

District, calls "weeding the garden." "Being focused is a key part of Wooster's improvement strategy," said Tefs, who credits the Ohio Improvement Process with providing the framework for eliminating fragmentation and improving coherence across the district. Reducing fragmentation through a guiding set of beliefs, and finding the right balance between accountability and empowerment also characterizes Gwinnett County Public Schools' approach to improvement.

In addition to reducing the number of priorities, districts were systematic in how they represented that core work and communicated it to the schools across the system. In all cases, a district plan—framed around a limited number of goals or strategies—guided the work of all schools. "We used to have many goals; now we are more strategically focused," explained Dr. Walt Christy, Director of Secondary Programs for Brevard Public Schools. The district's transition from what was described as an "enormous plan" to a few important goals provided a framework for aligning priorities in real ways. The same transformation to a more focused approach occurred in Tigard-Tualatin, where district and school personnel describe a similar change. "We've come a long way from having a long list of goals to focusing on one or two high-leverage actions that impact core instruction, and having fewer and fewer goals at the school level," said Dan Goldman. Kraig Sproles, Principal of Tigard-Tualatin's Metzger Elementary School, explained that "grade level goals are aligned to school goals, and school goals are aligned to district goals. We had idiosyncratic goals, and while they were sometimes good, there was no coherence across schools in the district. We've worked toward shared goals."

Focusing the work also means being intentional in how those

few priority areas are used to make decisions about resources. "The district strategic plan drives what we do and how we use resources. We're learning to focus on fewer things and do them well," said Dr. Beth Thedy, Assistant Superintendent of Student Services for Brevard Public Schools. The intentional use of resources—defined to include not only money, but also personnel, programs, and time—to achieve focused goals is also a theme in the Val Verde Unified School District. Dr. Michelle Richardson, former Assistant Superintendent for Business Services, described making the decisions about the use of funds as a collaborative process. "We looked at our data and prioritized where to put the dollars to drive the right work," said Richardson.

In SAU 56, personnel are committed to using available resources in more effective ways. "We're not going to add resources. We're looking differently at the use of time, and have unified professional development in terms of focusing on improvements in reading, mathematics, and behavior," explained Bob Marquis, Assistant Superintendent.

Another outcome of gaining the kind of focus needed to make and sustain district-wide improvements is the movement away from developing and implementing programs often used by a department or area within the district to an emphasis on identifying and implementing essential practices across all classrooms within all schools. "We don't develop programs in isolation," said Troy Knudsvig, Special Education Director for Val Verde Unified. Superintendent Mosca shares a similar philosophy. "We're clear about the district's focus. We're about improving instruction and addressing the needs of all children by providing universal instruction to all kids; it's not about programs," she said.

SELECT AND IMPLEMENT
SHARED INSTRUCTIONAL PRACTICES

Researchers have concluded that a specific focus on instructional practices is an important tool in improving performance for students. We've known for quite some time that not all instructional practices are of equal value (Hattie, 2009, 2012). In addition, there is a clear consensus in the research regarding the need for districts to focus on both student achievement and the quality of the instructional practices used, including a commitment to using specific researched-based instructional practices (Robinson, 2011; Hattie, 2009, 2012; Leithwood and Seashore Louis, 2012; Togneri and Anderson, 2003; Simmons, 2006; Supovitz, 2006; Leithwood and Jantzi, 2008; MacIver and Farley-Ripple, 2008; Marzano and Waters, 2008).

The research literature on effective instructional practices is very well developed. It is important to realize that we know more than enough about high-quality instruction to act on this knowledge. Hattie (2009) says that what matters most in terms of student progress is "attending to personalizing the learning, getting greater precision about how students are progressing in this learning, and ensuring professional learning of the teachers about how and when to provide different or more effective strategies for teaching and learning" (p. 245).

The districts identified here all have a strong instructional focus grounded in both specific instructional practices and teacher teams who collaboratively work together to decide what to teach, how to most effectively teach, how to measure performance, and what to do when students are and are not successful. This ongoing self-assessment by teacher teams of the effectiveness of their own teaching is what results in continuous improvement for every student.

Harnessing the collective talent and energy of teachers in ways that allow them to inform each other's instructional practice is a common theme in all featured districts. Each district has established structures for aligning the work across levels of the district (e.g., district, school, teacher team). While the names, numbers, and types of teams, as well as the team composition, differ somewhat across districts, the commitment to engaging *everyone* in continuous learning is evident. "Breaking down isolated practice and raising the capacity of the entire system of 850 teachers through collaborative teaming is a substantial cost to the district, but one that is necessary for improving learning for all students," said Michael McCormick, Val Verde's Assistant Superintendent for Educational Services.

In the Tigard-Tualatin School District, a similar commitment to consistent district-wide implementation of agreed-on strategies related to the district's effective behavior and instructional support model is evident and is supported through aligned team protocols and guidelines. "Individual teacher discretion or choosing your own adventure is not a good thing," explained Tiffany Wiencken, Principal of Deer Creek Elementary School. "Instead of trying different things and seeing if they make a difference, the system in place here forces consistent, collective implementation. I had four new members of a six-member core team, and if we hadn't had the system in place, we would not have achieved the gains we did. I'm completely in awe of the system; there are no invisible kids here," said Wiencken. "There is not an 'except for' attitude here," added Petrea Hagen-Gilden, formerly the Director of Special Education and Director of Elementary Education.

In each of the featured districts, instruction is viewed as the district's core work and developing common vocabulary for what constitutes high-quality instructional practice is an ongoing endeavor. For example, SAU 56 communicates clear expectations around priorities. "Improving the quality of academic and behavioral instruction *is* the work of the district," said Marquis. "There have been major shifts in the way we do instruction and in the system-wide attitude. It's about instruction," said Sandy Crockett, Reading Consultant at Maple Wood Elementary School.

In the Bartholomew Consolidated School District, Universal Design for Learning (UDL) is used as the district's instructional framework, providing the mechanism for staff to participate in a common, collective approach to meeting the needs of all youngsters and allowing the district to "move from engaging in random acts of improvement to really being focused and aligned," said Van Horn. "UDL has given us the common language and prompts, and has allowed us to look at what a child *can* do," said Gail Koors, sixth-grade teacher at Richards Elementary School.

In Stoughton Area School District, the focus on improving teaching and learning for all groups of students was aided through staff members' work on developing clear and aligned learning targets for each grade level. "The learning targets provided the basis for guiding formative and summative evaluation, providing feedback to students and parents, and designing, implementing, and monitoring interventions," explained Judy Singletary, Director of Curriculum and Instructional Services.

"Getting the right people in the right seats" is a theme of the Bloom Vernon Local Schools, whose administration has focused heavily on building the capacity of all staff members to meet the instructional needs of all children. Having high expectations for every child is a core belief guiding all personnel decisions. In Lake Villa, regardless of where a staff member "sits," he or she will be required to participate as a learning team member. "We do not support a 'menu' approach to professional development," said Barbour. Instead, Lake Villa district leadership has focused the district's work using the Data Teams process as the primary strategy for implementing agreed-on strategies across the district. This focused approach necessitates having all staff be knowledgeable and fully engaged in the Data Teams process. To that end, both Barbour and Superintendent Van Pelt are certified by The Leadership and Learning Center as Data Teams trainers and have personally trained every staff member in the district in the effective use of data by groups of teachers (i.e., learning teams).

In these districts, the superintendents are actively involved in leading the district improvement work. They not only set the direction but also are involved in monitoring and evaluating the progress of this work. "The superintendent cannot be a spectator; he/she must make clear that the work is the priority of the district," added Van Pelt. This sentiment is echoed by Superintendent Tefs in Wooster, Ohio. Wooster teachers are involved as members of teacher-based teams (TBTs), which are similar to Lake Villa's learning teams. And the work of the TBTs is aligned with the work of school-based teams (called building leadership teams) and the district leadership team. "I think the biggest culture shift has been the changing role of the central office, from one that controlled the work to a decentralized approach that works with and supports the implementation of shared practices in every school," said Tefs.

Like other project districts, Brevard Public Schools ensures that all teachers are trained in the use of the district's chosen improvement strategies—in Brevard's case, they're called "Brevard's Effective Strategies for Teachers" (BEST). Brevard also supports continuous improvement in instructional practice through the increasing use of professional learning communities as a way to embed ongoing professional development and promote shared instructional practices within and across schools. In the Gwinnett County Public Schools, a certain amount of flexibility is allowed at the school level. However, all schools must implement the district's improvement process and use research-based instructional practices, which are collectively referred to as "Quality-Plus Teaching Strategies."

IMPLEMENT DEEPLY

Deep implementation is a must. Douglas Reeves found that "half-hearted implementation was actually worse than minimal or no implementation" (Reeves, 2010, p. 36). Unless implementation reaches the 90 percent level, outcomes that are reported in the research cannot be expected. Having said this, it is probably fair to say that most schools and districts don't meet this 90 percent implementation standard. In most schools and districts, there is a large gap between the perceived levels of implementation (i.e., how well employees think initiatives are being implemented) versus the actuality of how well initiatives are being implemented. The biggest challenge we face today in education is our failure to implement well.

Deep implementation requires:

• Focusing on the shared learning of a few important things.

• Increasing the effectiveness of ongoing professional

development, including opportunities for feedback, ongoing practice, and coaching.

• A high level of monitoring, feedback, and support.

The districts identified here focused on two primary approaches for improvement:

1. Learning and deeply implementing specific effective instructional strategies.

2. The use of teams at the classroom, school, and district levels.

These two approaches were the primary focus for their improvement work. However, the most effective improvements to instruction (i.e., learning, applying, and practicing powerful instructional practices) were accomplished through the development of teacher-based instructional teams. These districts found that having a focus on powerful instructional practices paired with opportunities for practice in their teacher teams enabled them to make progress with all of their students, including students with disabilities.

In the Wooster City School District, implementation rubrics are used to support deeper levels of implementation of agreed-upon strategies and actions—all designed to reach the district's established goals. Similarly, in Brevard Public Schools, a variety of measures are used to continually assess the degree of implementation of strategies across the district and whether that implementation is having the desired effect on student learning. The notion of "less is more," or limiting the number of priority areas (as described above), allows for deeper implementation of fewer strategies/actions that can leverage change.

Balancing fidelity of implementation with flexibility to meet student needs is an ongoing conversation in many of the districts. Professional development serves an important purpose in supporting full implementation of identified strategies. For example, in the Bartholomew Consolidated School Corporation, professional development is provided to all personnel on the consistent use of Universal Design for Learning and, in fact, all district-designed professional development must be grounded in UDL. In the Tigard-Tualatin School District, deeper implementation of the district's effective behavior and instructional support strategies is also supported by the district's intentional use of school psychologists. Dan Goldman explains: "Before, every elementary school had 1.0 counselors and 0.25 school psychologists. Now, as counselors retire, the positions are filled with school psychologists who provide counseling and other services, not only assessment for special education eligibility."

In Stoughton Area School District, school psychologists and speech-language pathologists work with teachers to co-implement instruction for all students. For example, at Sandhill Elementary School, Counselor Abby Fritz works alongside Title 1 Learning Strategist Jennifer Hopper and classroom teachers to align intervention to student needs and conduct daily formative assessment. Andrea Wilke, who teaches third grade and works closely with Fritz and others, says, "I believe in having all kids supported in my classroom; we're using adults better."

At Kegonsa Elementary School, School Psychologist Samantha Rogers fulfills a similar role. "Sam is key; she's visible in the classroom and serves as a coteacher in many ways. It's an investment for the district to do that," remarked Julie Alexander, who teaches first grade.

At the elementary level, the cross-categorical alignment of learning strategists assigned to support the instructional process for students with disabilities, students identified as talented/gifted, and students who are English language learners (ELLs) has allowed for greater integration of services/supports while strengthening collaboration across roles. Integrating service delivery around learning targets has "allowed us to develop a common vocabulary and support the transition from a focus on teaching to a focus on learning," said Fox Prairie Elementary School kindergarten teacher Mary Tullis.

At the high school level, learning strategists (special education teachers) are assigned to content-area teams so that they develop a deeper understanding of grade-level expectations, and can therefore support deeper implementation of agreed-on instructional strategies in meeting the needs of all learners. "Consistency is huge. At the beginning, I [worked] across all content areas," said Learning Strategist Stephen Stokes. Now, rather than working across all content areas, Stokes, like other learning strategists at the high school, are assigned to a departmental content-area team. This organizational scheme makes it possible for learning strategists to learn their assigned content well, positioning them to better meet the instructional needs of all students. "Since learning strategists are in the regular classrooms as part of our department, they've become advisors to the entire department and the students see them not as special education teachers, but as a teacher; all of us work with all kids," said Science Team Advisor Cindy Carter.

Deeper implementation of core work was supported in SAU 56 through the thoughtful and intentional use of guidance on implementation stages and drivers, which is provided through

State Implementation & Scaling-up of Evidence-Based Practices (SISEP) Center. Awareness of what it takes to reach full implementation, and systematically incorporating checks along the way to facilitate a common understanding of what full implementation looks like, are among the strategies used by the district.

MONITOR, PROVIDE FEEDBACK, AND PROVIDE SUPPORT

Monitoring means focusing on the follow-through of "adult actions," i.e., are the adults following through on their implementation of the agreed-upon practices? Reeves (2010) found that districts and schools that scored high in monitoring, evaluation, and inquiry had gains that were two to fives times greater than schools and districts that scored lower on these dimensions. In these studies, "monitoring" meant that there was frequent (at least monthly) analysis by the teams of the following:

- The use of specific teaching strategies.
- Formative student performance data.
- The use of leadership practices that supported the implementation.

Currently, most districts don't collect data on their implementation effectiveness, so they don't really know how well they are implementing. This makes it extremely difficult to know whether they are making progress as a district or not.

Monitoring requires that we have some way of collecting data on the level and quality of implementation. Effective schools and districts know how well they are implementing their improvement work. It is critical that everyone understands that the purpose of monitoring is to collect and analyze data to provide feedback and to assess how well the implementation strategies (i.e., training, coaching, modeling, etc.) are working, not to punish people. Fullan (2008) is quick to warn us that negative monitoring does not work.

Monitoring helps us to determine where our implementation is successful and where we need more support. Monitoring data is an important barometer in terms of our "reciprocal accountability." If individuals or teams are struggling with their implementation, can they— and do they—seek support and suggestions from other sources? Reciprocal accountability means that each person and each team are responsible for each other's success. It is critical to understand that individuals and teams need differential kinds and levels of support if they are going to successfully implement new practices well. These kinds of support are particularly evident in the districts identified here.

Val Verde Unified uses a variety of tactics to monitor the degree of implementation of agreed-upon strategies across the district, and to strengthen the skills of all staff in improving the achievement of all students. District leaders regularly conduct classroom observations, looking for trends, and meet with principals and teachers to identify ways in which the central office can better support schools. "There's an umbrella here, and we've got schools covered. If you don't feed the teachers, they eat the students. People need feedback, and they feel supported because they see us," said Michelle Richardson.

Technology, coupled with effective data use, is used in districts to support more systematic monitoring of implementation. Grade-level teams meet regularly and often to monitor student progress and performance.

In SAU 56, the district's leadership team assesses the degree to which schools are building capacity to meet the instructional needs of all children, and to provide feedback to principals, teachers, and others across the district. Principal walk-throughs are commonly used to gather data on predetermined instructional strategies that should be implemented across classrooms. "We know what we're looking for," said Marquis.

In the Wooster City School District, in addition to evaluating the impact that key strategies are having on student learning, the effectiveness of the district and building leadership teams is evaluated on an ongoing basis to ensure that improvements are made continually. All Wooster teams complete the district leadership team and building leadership team effectiveness surveys. "One of our biggest successes has involved taking six elementary schools and making them more alike than different in terms of the quality and consistency of instruction being provided to all kids," said Tefs.

The superintendent of Tigard-Tualatin demanded that whatever was agreed on and/or adopted had to be implemented with 100 percent fidelity across the district. "I felt that key actions needed to be implemented across schools so we could make decisions about what needed to be done and what was not working," said former district Superintendent Rob Saxton, now Deputy Superintendent of Public Instruction for the state of Oregon. "We took a hard line on the use of data and teaming—everyone had to do it—and the results were ridiculously good. It was hard to argue with them," said Goldman.

Improving the quality and consistency of instruction for all children, and learning from what Bartholomew's Jensen calls "structured failure" so that effective practice is replicated across the district, is a goal of the district's continuous improvement process. The use of monitoring tools, such as the district's Universal Design for Learning (UDL) rubrics and supports, increases teachers' and related services providers' understanding (see Exhibit 7.4).

"It's the consistent and persistent conversations that teachers have around working with, understanding, and challenging the [UDL] framework, and the impact on student learning, that lead to growth," said former UDL Coordinator Dr. Loui Lord-Nelson.

BOOK FIVE EXHIBIT 7.4   **Excerpt from Bartholomew UDL Rubric**

BCSC UDL RUBRIC • Excerpt

UDL Principle	UDL Teaching Method	Not Yet Evident	Emerging	Inter-mediate	Advanced
Multiple means of represen-tation	Provide multiple media formats	Students are only given one resource, such as a textbook.	The teacher locates several (1–2) resources, such as books of different reading difficulty.	The teacher locates several (2–3) resources, such as books and websites of different reading dificulty	The **teacher and students** locate several (4–5) resources, such as videos and books and websites of different reading difficulty. The materials are then made available digitally as well as on audiotape for flexible accessibility.

Source: Rose, Meyer, and Hitchcock, 2005.

INQUIRE AND LEARN

Hargreaves and Fullan (2012) state that "what is needed is a profession that constantly and collectively builds its knowledge base and corresponding expertise, where practices and their impact are transparently tested, developed, circulated, and adapted. There needs to be a continuous amalgamation of precision and innovation, as well as inquiry, improvisation, and experimentation" (p. 50).

Schools and districts that make continuous progress create systems, structures, and supports; an active inquiry process; and follow-up actions that are grounded in data, analysis, reflection, and learning. Using more powerful research-based teaching practices and the use of teacher-based teams can result in improved outcomes, but only if individuals and teams can learn and apply that learning to make continuous progress.

Darling-Hammond (2010) sees this change in the way we view accountability as a new and emerging paradigm for schools and districts. "In this new paradigm the design of the school district office should also evolve from a set of silos that rarely interact with one another to a team structure. . . . This means they must continuously evaluate how schools are doing, seeking to learn from successful schools and to support improvement in struggling schools by ensuring that these schools secure strong leadership and excellent teachers, and are supported in adopting successful program strategies. Districts will need to become learning organizations themselves—developing their capacity to investigate and learn from innovation in order to leverage productive strategies and develop their capacity to support successful change" (p. 271).

Elmore (2006) says that improving instruction requires continuous and collective learning on the part of every person in the system. He states that "the existing institutional structure of public education does one thing very well: it creates a normative environment that values idiosyncratic, isolated, and individualistic learning at the expense of collective learning. The existing system does not value continuous learning as a collective good and does not make this learning the individual and social responsibility of every member of the system. Leaders must create environments in which individuals expect to have their personal ideas and practices subjected to the scrutiny of their colleagues. Privacy of practice produces isolation; isolation is the enemy of improvement" (p. 67).

By working collectively and collaboratively using data, focusing goals and strategies, improving instruction, identifying the successes and challenges of implementation, and monitoring and providing feedback, the district-, building- and teacher-based Data Teams can develop a deeper sense of how to facilitate learning at every level. As Fullan (2008) says, "Learning is the work," and organizational learning must become the engine of sustainability (Supovitz, 2006).

The districts discussed here have all found ways to continuously inquire and learn from their progress.

In the Gwinnett County Public Schools, the three Cs—continuity, consistency, and courageous behavior—are the watchwords of the district's ongoing efforts to meet the instructional needs of each student. According to Dr. Glenn Pethel, Executive Director of Leadership Development, "Sustained progress is key. If you're using your data and turning it into information that allows you to make better instructional decisions, all children—whether they're students with disabilities, English language learners, or children typically thought of as regular education students—will benefit from the district's focus on instruction and learning."

In Lake Villa, a well-established culture of inquiry is evident at each level across the district—from the central office, to schools, to classrooms. "We need to be able to connect results to specific action steps. We wouldn't be able to do that if schools worked in isolation," explained Barbour. "How principals are evaluated is key," according to Van Pelt. "Principals are, and are expected to be, part of a larger conversation about instruction and achievement beyond what happens in their individual school," he added. Similarly, Brevard Public Schools requires principals, teachers, and central office personnel to work together to meet the district's strategy of "leadership and job-related capacity at every level of the organization." In fact, the district incorporated employee learning as a required and monitored part of the evaluation process.

That same kind of collective commitment to and responsibility for the success of all children in the district is evident in SAU 56. "We're past finger pointing, especially at the middle and high school levels, in terms of who to blame for student failure. Now, all staff need to be responsible for all kids," said Kate Segal, Somersworth Middle School Assistant Principal.

Another aspect of becoming a learning organization involves adults in the system holding each other accountable for student learning. "All adults in all buildings are responsible for all children. It's not a thing you have to do; it is evidence of our core beliefs," said Singletary, of the Stoughton Area School District. In Val Verde Unified, "Everyone knows their role in kids' lives and everyone wants to be here," said Marie-Antoinette McPhee, Assistant Principal of Rancho Verde High School.

The phrase "Val Verde Way" is used by personnel to refer to the district's culture, nurtured through a longstanding commitment to relationship building, support, and collective ownership. "The Val Verde Way means that each member of the community is part of something important—the chance to affect the lives of children. The culture rubs off on the kids," said Jim Owens, Principal of March Middle School. "Success is a motivator; it spirals up," said Bloom Vernon's Johnson.

SUMMARY

The Moving Your Numbers project showcased the work of 10 districts with dramatically different demographics to identify specific practices that contributed to higher levels of student, adult, and organizational learning. The resulting case studies offer existence proofs, demonstrating that it *is* possible to make a positive difference for all learners—including those identified as special education students, English language learners, and others characterized as "high need"—as part of overall district improvement and reform efforts. While the conclusions provided through this work are limited to the districts featured, these districts share many of the same demographics and characteristics of a large number of districts across the country.

The six practices identified here have been effective across a variety of districts, and specifically benefit students with disabilities. As schools and districts struggle to meet the needs of increasingly diverse learners, it is important to find strategies that result in the progress of all students. We hope that sharing the results of the districts highlighted here will allow wider replication of the use of these practices and result in better achievement for all students.

References

Darling-Hammond, L. (2010). *The flat world and education: How America's commitment to equity will determine our future.* New York, NY: Teachers College Press.

Elmore, R. F. (2006). *School reform from the inside out: Policy, practice, and performance.* Cambridge, MA: Harvard Education Press.

Fullan, M. (2008). *The six secrets of change: What the best leaders do to help their organizations survive and thrive.* San Francisco, CA: Jossey-Bass.

Fullan, M. (Ed.). (2009). *The challenge of change: Start school improvement now* (2nd ed.). Thousand Oaks, CA: Corwin.

Hargreaves, A., & Fullan, M. (2012). *Professional capitol: Transforming teaching in every school.* New York, NY: Teachers College Press.

Hattie, J. (2009). *Visible learning: A synthesis of over 800 meta-analyses relating to achievement.* New York, NY: Routledge.

Hattie, J. (2012). *Visible learning for teachers: Maximizing impact on learning.* New York, NY: Routledge.

Leithwood, K., & Jantzi, D. (2008). Linking leadership to student learning: The contributions of leader efficacy. *Educational Administration Quarterly, 44,* 496.

Leithwood, K., & Seashore Louis, K. (2012). *Linking leadership to student learning.* San Francisco, CA: Jossey-Bass.

Levin, B. (2009). Reform without (much) rancor. In A. Hargreaves & M. Fullan (Eds.), *Change wars.* Bloomington, IN: Solution Tree.

MacIver, M. A., & Farley-Ripple, E. (2008). *Bringing the district back in: The role of the central office in instruction and achievement.* Baltimore, MD: Center for Research on the Education of Students Placed at Risk.

Marzano, R. J., & Waters, T. (2008). *District leadership that works: Striking the right balance.* Bloomington, IN: Solution Tree.

McNulty, B. A., & Besser, L. (2011). *Leaders make it happen: An administrator's guide to data teams.* Englewood, CO: Lead + Learn Press.

Reeves, D. B. (2009). Level-five networks: Mmaking significant change in complex organizations. In A. Hargreaves & M. Fullan (Eds.), *Change wars.* Bloomington, IN: Solution Tree.

Reeves, D. B. (2010). *Transforming professional development into student results.* Alexandria, VA: ASCD.

Reeves, D. B. (2011). *Finding your leadership focus: What matters most for student results.* New York, NY: Teachers College Press.

Robinson, V. (2011). *Student-centered leadership.* San Francisco, CA: Jossey-Bass.

Rose, D. H., Meyer, A., & Hitchcock, C. (Eds.). (2005). *The universally designed classroom: Accessible curriculum and digital technologies.* Cambridge, MA: Harvard Education Press.

Schmoker, M. J. (2011). *Focus: Elevating the essentials to radically improve student outcomes.* Alexandria, VA: ASCD.

Simmons, J. (2006). *Breaking through: Transforming urban schools.* Amsterdam, NY: Teacher College Press.

Supovitz, J. A. (2006). *The case for district-based reform: Leading, building, and sustaining school improvement.* Cambridge, MA: Harvard Education Press.

Telfer, D. M. (2011). *Moving your numbers: Five districts share how they used assessment and accountability to increase performance for students with disabilities as part of district-wide improvement.* Minneapolis, MN: University of Minnesota, National Center on Educational Outcomes.

Togneri, W., & Anderson, S. E. (2003). *Beyond islands of excellence: What districts can do to improve instruction and achievement in all schools—A leadership brief* (Stock No. 303369). Washington, DC: Learning First Alliance.

Index